THE AUDIENCE, THE MESSAGE, THE SPEAKER

THE AUDIENCE, THE MESSAGE, THE SPEAKER

FIFTH EDITION

John Hasling

Foothill College

McGraw-Hill, Inc.

New York   St. Louis   San Francisco   Auckland   Bogotá   Caracas
Lisbon   London   Madrid   Mexico   Milan   Montreal
New Delhi   Paris   San Juan   Singapore   Sydney   Tokyo   Toronto

This book was set in Times Roman by Arcata Graphics/Kingsport.
The editors were Hilary Jackson, Fran Marino, and Tom Holton;
the production supervisor was Denise L. Puryear.
The cover was designed by Warren Infield.
The photo editor was Debra Hershkowitz.
Arcata Graphics/Halliday was printer and binder.

Cover Photos Credits (left to right):
Sepp Seitz, Woodfin Camp & Associates
Superstock
Jodi Buren, Woodfin Camp & Associates

THE AUDIENCE, THE MESSAGE, THE SPEAKER

1 2 3 4 5 6 7 8 9 0   HAL HAL   9 0 9 8 7 6 5 4 3 2

ISBN 0-07-026999-8

Library of Congress Cataloging-in-Publication Data

Hasling, John.
    The audience, the message, the speaker / John Hasling,—5th ed.
      p.   cm.
    Rev. ed. of: The message, the speaker, the audience. 4th ed. New York:
McGraw-Hill, c1988.
    Includes index.
    ISBN 0-07-026999-8
    1. Public speaking.   I. Hasling, John.   Message, the speaker, the
audience.   II. Title.
PN4121.H267   1993
808.5'1—dc20   92-15896

ABOUT
THE AUTHOR

John (Jack) Hasling is a professor of speech communication at Foothill College in Los Altos Hills, California. He received his M.A. from Sacramento State University in 1963 where he later became a lecturer in speech and coach of the debate team. In 1966 he moved to Foothill College and has taught there ever since. His primary area of expertise is in public address, but he also teaches courses in group discussion, interpersonal communication, and radio broadcasting. In his earlier years he had worked as an announcer and engineer at several northern California radio stations acquiring experience that enabled him to write a textbook entitled *Fundamentals of Radio Broadcasting,* which was published by McGraw-Hill in 1980.

In addition to teaching, John Hasling has been actively involved in faculty affairs at the state and local level. He served as chairperson of the Foothill College Improvement of Instruction Committee and later as president of the Academic Senate. He is a former member of the Commission on Instruction for the California Association of Community Colleges and is a charter member of the Bay Area Speech Teachers Association. He has also served twice as parliamentarian at the California State Academic Senate convention.

To Elsie for her gentle
and insightful critiques

CONTENTS

PREFACE

Students who say they have had no experience in public speaking may be forgetting about the times they spent as a member of the audience. It would be difficult to imagine an adult who had never been to a lecture, church service, court trial, panel discussion, travelogue, or pep rally. Any of those occasions can be used as a model for studying public speaking. The principles we teach in speech classes come to us from observations that are made by members of the audience. The view from that perspective, therefore, seems to be the logical starting place for a course in public address—thus, the sequence, The Audience, the Message, and the Speaker.

CULTURAL ENRICHMENT

In Chapter 1 I have also presented a brief list of historic orators who have profoundly influenced the way people of the world have reacted to the events and issues of their times. My main purpose for doing this was to illustrate the power of the spoken word, but there are other reasons for including such a list: It serves as an opportunity for instructors to introduce students to at least a fragment of information that is essential for a liberal arts education. This might be regarded as tangential to some students and may prompt them to ask the inevitable question, "Why do I need to know about these things?" Sometimes I say, "Because your audience will know about them and you should too"; however, that is not an altogether satisfactory response. A student who wants to learn public speaking in order to become a ski instructor may regard the connection between parallel turns and Greek philosophy to be rather remote. The fact is that a liberal arts education may indeed not be a necessary criterion for a ski instructor. If we were to view public speaking purely from a vocational perspective we would be able to reduce the subject matter of the course considerably. Libraries and bookstores are full of manuals that give nothing but practical information on techniques for delivering an effective speech. If I were to teach public speaking in a trade school or as an in-service training course for a large corporation, I'm sure I would teach it quite differently than I do in a college setting.

Throughout the text, therefore, I have made an intentional effort to include what might be called a "value added" element to the subject matter. Whenever possible I have tried to use examples that would do more than simply illustrate the point pertaining to rhetorical style or methodology; I have attempted to sneak in cultural references that I believe are important for all speakers to know. In Chapter 7, "Thinking and Reasoning," I have elaborated on this point of view. The value of conclusions drawn by speakers on current social issues is dependent not only on their reasoning process, but also on their understanding of related historical and cultural information. A speech course at the college level should require that students know something about government, world and national history, literature, science, and the arts. My hope is that this text will at least identify a few fundamentals of cultural literacy.

CRITICAL THINKING

As speech instructors we are in the business of teaching more than just communication skills; our charge is to foster the development of critical thinking. Before students can deliver a speech persuasively they must first be able to reach a sensible conclusion of their own based on reliable evidence. In this edition I have continued to use the syllogism as a basic tool of reasoning because it is well designed for teaching important and relevant social principles as well as logic. For example, the claim in a major premise might be that every person charged with a crime is entitled to due process of law. A statement of that kind calls attention to constitutional rights and also demonstrates the rule of logic that the same conclusion must be drawn for anyone who falls into that category.

CONTENT AND ORGANIZATION

The infrastructure of any speech textbook is, of course, its sections on gathering and organizing information. Students need to know where to find facts and how to put them together. In this edition I have responded to the requests of reviewers to include a sample speech that is strong in content and has a clear organizational structure. The presentation by

Thomas Kuhn that you will find in the appendix is one that I believe students will enjoy reading, not just because it is a good model, but also because it contains an abundance of "interest grabbers"—pertinent bits of information that entertain as well as educate.

ATTITUDES AND ETHICS

The speech teacher who has to get four or five rounds of speeches into the course may be too burdened by time constraints to delve very deeply into psychological and philosophical elements of oral communication. I recognize that problem because it is a frustrating one for me too. For this reason, I rely on the text that I use to expose students to material upon which I am not able to elaborate in class. I try, however, to point out connections for them to see. The value of the principles expressed in Chapter 11, "Meeting Ethical Standards," depends to a large extent on students being willing to accept assertions which I have made in other parts of the textbook. Aristotle claims, for example, that good sense is a criterion for good ethics. Therefore, developing a clear thinking and reasoning process is a necessary pursuit for meeting ethical standards as well as for becoming an effective speaker. But there is still another connection I like to make—relating ethical standards to speech anxiety. I believe that good ethics contributes to high self-esteem, and therefore to better performance on the podium. The person who can openly and honestly express the reasoning behind his or her claims without feeling defensive or anxious about audience criticism is a person who will be able to speak with confidence. But people who have hidden motives based on greed, prejudice, or selfish interests are going to be inclined to speak obtusely in order to avoid public scrutiny. In addition to all the other advantages, a speech course which emphasizes ethical considerations contributes in a very positive way to good mental health.

ACKNOWLEDGMENTS

The opportunity to revise this text has been a gratifying experience for me in terms of my own personal and professional growth. I would like to thank the editorial staff at McGraw-Hill, particularly Fran Marino and Hilary Jackson. And I am sincerely grateful for the valuable reviews that were written by Jerry Agent, Hinds Community College; Kenneth R. Albone, Glassboro State College; Stanley Crane, Hartnell Community College; Sam Edelman, California State University at Chico; Dennis Fus, University of Nebraska at Omaha; Walter Johnson, Cumberland Community College; and Robert Payne, East Central University.

John Hasling

PART **ONE**

THE AUDIENCE

CHAPTER 1

THE COMMUNICATION PROCESS

A writer, a book, and a reader provide a communication model. It is a basic and fairly simple model, but it is one that is useful for us to examine. It consists of a sender, a message, and a receiver—the three elements that are essential in order for human communication to take place. My task as the sender of the message is to present ideas in ways that make it possible for you to receive and understand them; your task is to interpret what you think I mean. The model is a simple one because I am not getting any immediate response from you. If we were in the same room, there would be another dimension, because messages would be flowing in both directions. Even if you were not saying anything, I would be getting feedback that would tell me something about the way you were reacting. You might be doing nothing more than sitting in your room with the book open, but you would be exhibiting behavior patterns that I could observe. You might look up from time to time with a puzzled expression on your face; you might sigh, shake your head, nod, or perhaps even close the book altogether and turn on the TV. Those are all messages that I would be receiving and trying to interpret, just as you are trying to garner meaning from the words that I put on the page.

COMMUNICATION MODELS

When people relate to one another face to face, we say that the communication is *transactional:* That means there are messages flowing in both directions simultaneously; you and the other person are both senders and receivers.[1] The term *transactional* does not mean that each person is *talking* at the same time; messages do not have to be *verbal.* A great deal of the meaning that we convey to other people is in the form of *nonverbal* messages. When you smile and nod your head, you are saying, "I hear you, and I like what you say," just as clearly as you would if you were to speak the words. Often we forget that when we are in the presence of another person, we are sending messages whether we intend to or not; in fact, it is impossible for us *not* to communicate. Communication models can give you a picture of the process in which you participate every day of your life whether you are aware of it or not, and they can show you how components vary from one situation to another. If you understand the theory behind the practice, you will have a better chance of knowing how to be intentional in what you do and say.

Conversation Model

There are a number of communication models that we could examine. In an ordinary conversation we say that the communication is *unstructured*—there are no formalized requirements placed on any of the individuals to conform to any particular style, topic, or sequence. The only rules or guidelines that are imposed on people in a conversational mode are those that social convention and common courtesy require. A two-person model is not difficult to examine, but when there are several other people in the conversation, the dynamics become more complex (Figure 1–1). There may be one person in the group to whom you relate differently, and that variation may affect the way the others react to you. From your own expe-

[1] Sylvia Moss and Stewart L. Tubbs, *Human Communication,* 6th ed., McGraw-Hill, New York, 1991, pp. 6–7.

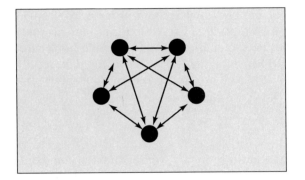

Figure 1
Unstructured
conversation
model.

rience in groups you are probably aware that what others do and say has a strong influence on your own behavior. If you perceive that people are interested and are listening to your ideas, you may elaborate more fully; if you believe they are bored or are disapproving, you might hold back or even say nothing at all. Probably the best conversations you have are those in which the participants regard each other as equals. When one person attempts to introduce structure to the conversation by leading or directing the flow of communication, the dynamics change and the model begins to take a different shape.

Group Discussion Model

People may get together in small groups for reasons that are purely social, but on other occasions there may be a specific task that members want to accomplish. A group with an identified purpose might be called a "committee" or a "task force" and probably would have an "agenda" so that members stick to the topic which they are supposed to be addressing. An agenda puts limitations on the subject matter and gives focus and direction to the discussion (Figure 1–2). There would probably be a specified time for the meeting to start and end; there would be goals that the group is expected to accomplish, and probably a summary statement at the end so the members would know what they had decided. Participants might make some preparation for a discussion of this kind, but they would speak in an impromptu fashion—that is, they would not plan their remarks in advance, and they would not expect to speak in any particular order.

Public Speaking Model

A third model of communication is a situation in which one person has the attention of many others for an extended period of time. This is the

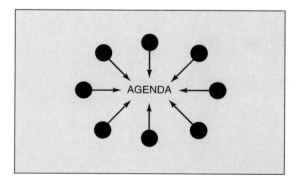

Figure 2
Group discussion model.

model that is generally referred to as *public speaking* (Figure 1–3). There are a number of reasons why this model is significantly different from those previously mentioned.

Structure   First of all, a speech delivered to an audience is a *structured* message. That means the speaker has some sort of organizational framework in mind and has given thought to how the message will start, how the ideas will be developed, and what conclusion will be drawn at the end. The speaker will make an effort to focus on a central theme and not drift off onto unrelated tangents. Also there is probably an expectation that the audience will hear the message all the way through to the end before they interrupt with their own remarks. These are characteristics that would not be appropriate for a person participating in a social conversation or group discussion.

Purpose   In a public speaking class, I teach my students to maintain consistency in their *purpose* while they are on the platform. If they are advocating a particular point of view, they are to defend that position even if they get objections from members of the audience. It is inappropriate for a speaker to make structural modifications of a thesis while standing on the podium. Qualifications that need to be made in a speaker's main purpose should be thought of *before* the audience has invested the time it takes to hear a speech. Certainly it is true that dialogue is a source of information and ideas, and thinking people should be able and willing to adjust their opinions in response to new evidence, but dialogue is a communication model that is quite different from public speaking. If your thoughts and ideas are still in the formative stage, try them out in conversations with your friends and in small groups; make whatever changes need be made before you advance your claims to an audience in a public speaking situation.

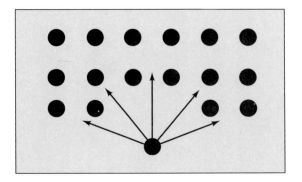

Figure 3
Public speaking model.

Posture   In public speaking we *stand* when we speak. Adopting this posture may be the very thing you dislike most about that mode of communication, but there is a very good reason for it: When we address an audience, we want to be the focus of attention. Standing is a nonverbal message that means "I have the floor and I want you to listen until I am finished." Sitting down is an invitation for others to speak. There is an expectation on the part of the audience that the person who is standing has something to say that is worthy of attention and wants to be heard.

Motivation   One of the most important differences between public speaking and conversation is the motivation of the speaker. You converse with your friends because you enjoy the experience. You are not doing it for *their* benefit; you are doing for your own. When you make a presentation, you may still be enjoying the experience (certainly you want your audience to believe that you are), but it's the audience's interest that you serve more than your own. You don't stand up in front of a group of people because you have a burning desire to give a speech. You do it because you believe you have information that will be useful to those who hear it. That may be an important notion for you to keep in mind on those occasions when you really don't want to subject yourself to the anxiety of addressing an audience.

MAKING OURSELVES UNDERSTOOD

Let's go back to our basic model of communication. As the writer of these words, I have no way of knowing whether or not my message is getting through to you. It might be that someone else is trying to talk to you while you are reading; you might have put the book down by this time and perhaps are engaged in something totally unrelated to the words on this page. You may still have the book in your lap, but your thoughts could be a million miles away.

Noise

In communication theory, anything that detracts from your receiving a message is called *noise*. Noise can be of a physical nature such as a smoky room that is causing you discomfort or a television program that you can see out of the corner of your eye and are trying to watch while you are reading the book. In a public speaking situation it might be distractions caused by members of the audience rattling chairs, or a faulty sound system that squeals when the volume is turned up. Noise can also be of a psychological nature. For example, you may resent the fact that you have been assigned to read this chapter when there are other things you would much rather be doing, or there may be references in the book that remind you of unpleasant experiences which are difficult for you to put out of your mind. Psychological noise could be any emotional feeling that competes with the cognitive reception of the message. Both the sender and the receiver could be aware of physical noise, but only the receiver would be affected by psychological noise.

Feedback

If I were in the same room with you trying to explain what I mean, our communication would be transactional. I would be able to observe physical noise distractions that might be interfering with your reception of the message, and I would be able to receive your verbal and the nonverbal feedback. You might just nod your head as I talk, or you could respond verbally and say, "I know what you mean." If you had any difficulty in comprehending, you could say, "I don't understand that." Feedback is a very important part of the communication process because it makes it possible for the sender to correct for error or add clarification to the message.

Language

When I write, I use words to convey my meaning, and my assumption is that you as the reader will have an understanding of those words. But even if we both speak the same language, I can never be sure that we attach the same meaning to the words. A few paragraphs back I used the word *dialogue* as a communication model that was different from public speaking. When I wrote the word, I pictured in my mind two people in face-to-face conversation discussing an issue. But the meaning of the word *dialogue* is not limited to the picture that I have in my mind. *Dialogue* is a term used in theater to mean the lines that people speak on the stage. You could also say that you have an ongoing dialogue with a friend who lives many miles away. We might not even be talking about people: Two organizations or institutions could maintain a business dialogue. Observations of this kind lead us to the conclusion that words can contain different meaning for different people. One meaning is contained in the mind of the person who initiates the message, but the same word may have a different meaning to the receiver. In "The Walrus and the Carpenter," Lewis Carroll observes the foolishness of Humpty-Dumpty, who says, "When I use a word, it means just what I choose it to mean—neither more nor less." Our attempts to communicate would be pointless if we did not consider the importance of the way the message is received.

Another way of viewing the complexities of language is to say that words have both denotative and connotative meaning. The denotative meaning is that which we find in the dictionary and forms the basis for our understanding. The connotative meaning refers to subjective interpretations that are attached to words. I might say of a speaker that he was very *forceful* in his delivery, meaning that his arguments were convincing and he was confident in what he was saying. The connotations that you attach to the word *forceful* might be that the person was arrogant and abrasive.

Almost all words have connotations; that means that we can never count on our own interpretation's being exactly the same as that of the person whom we are addressing. Only in physics and mathematics do we find symbols that have singular meanings, but even then there are sometimes variations. You might say that the names of the elements are not subject to interpretation; however, *gold* is an element, and that certainly is a word which means different things to different people. The elements sodium and chlorine seem to have stable meanings, but when they are combined to form salt, we have a term that takes on connotations. A person who is an "old salt" is not necessarily the "salt of the earth." The point is that words are not absolutes; they are *abstractions* that symbolize what we mean. When we examine symbols that convey meaning, we are not dealing with mathematics or physics, we are studying semantics.

Semantics

Language is an invention that evolved from human thought, and as such it is far from perfect. At best it is a tool that can be used with varying degrees of skill for communicating meaning. Semantics is the study of all ways in which meaning is conveyed. Linguistic communication is perhaps the most explicit method for making yourself understood, but by themselves words are often not completely adequate. We know that in oral communication volume and vocal inflection can alter meaning when we place emphasis on some words and not on others. From the visual perspective we are aware that posture, gesture, and facial expression influence the way our message is received.

If you have ever had to ask a question of a person unfamiliar with your language, you know that it is difficult, but not impossible, to convey what you want to say without verbalizing. When you are in such a situation, you probably rely on acting out the meaning as you would do if you were playing charades. If your question pertains to a physical object that is close at hand, you can point to it; if there is an action verb in the message, you can go through the motions. You may even resort to drawing a picture for the person. One form of nonverbal communication that may be familiar to

you is international signs that appear on highways and in public accommodations. Here we find an example of important messages that must be conveyed quickly and accurately, relying totally on the receiver's ability to interpret pictures. We call these *icons.*

In the case of a "no smoking" sign, the message is clear even though no words have been used. However, if you are trying to get across an abstract idea, your task is more difficult. Imagine, for example, that you wanted to ask the person who does not speak your language if the journey across the mountain would be *strenuous.* There is nothing you can point to that conveys the idea of "strenuous." Neither the sound nor the letters in the word have any relationship to the concept of strenuousness. Pronunciation of the word conveys meaning only to those who have been taught to associate the word with the idea. This is why we say that words are not containers of meaning; they are simply abstractions to which we assign meaning.

Operational Meaning

When I say that words are abstractions, I mean that there is nothing about the sounds I make or the marks on the page that is inherently connected to the thing I am describing. S. I. Hayakawa suggests that some words are more concrete than others and that they can be examined on a scale of abstraction.[2] For example I can use the word *cow* and be fairly confident that the image in my mind is quite similar to yours. When I use the expression *livestock,* there probably will be some differences. When I start to talk about *farm assets,* I am rather high on the scale of abstraction and the chances are that you do not have the same picture in your mind as I do in mine.

---

[2] S. I. Hayakawa, *Language in Thought and Action,* Harcourt, Brace & World, New York, 1949, pp. 168–170.

```
+-------------------------------------------------+
|            Scale of Abstraction                 |
|   More abstract      ▲    5 Farm assets         |
|                      │    4 Livestock           |
|                      │    3 Farm animals        |
|                      │    2 Dairy animals       |
|   Less abstract      ▼    1 Cow                 |
+-------------------------------------------------+
```

In the study of semantics we say that some word combinations have *operational meaning*—that means we are able to describe things in terms of size, weight, distance, volume, shape, number, or observable action. But when we get into the realm of aesthetic qualities, feelings, beliefs, values, categories, and concepts, we move higher up on the scale of abstraction.

Semantic Reactions

Communication is complex because we know that much of what we say does not have operational meaning. In many cases the best we can do is to create *semantic reactions*—generating either a favorable or an unfavorable response. If I have good communication skills, I should be able to get the kind of reaction from you that I want. If my intent is to have you think favorably about a person, I might say, "He is firmly committed to his beliefs." To create an unfavorable response I would probably say, "He is stubborn in his opinions." While the two statements may appear to be similar, the semantic reaction in one case would be significantly different from the other. This is a principle we must be able to understand in order to communicate effectively.

In political rhetoric we can find a great many examples of words and phrases that have worked to the advantage or to the disadvantage of candidates. A national debate was touched off in 1964 when Barry Goldwater made the claim that extremism in the cause of virtue was no vice. There were many people who reacted negatively to the phrase and branded Senator Goldwater as an "extremist." The word *liberal* played a significant part in the 1988 presidential campaign. Michael Dukakis and other Democratic contenders tried to disassociate themselves from the term, because nationwide it seemed to have taken on negative connotations. Language is used in a very powerful way to influence public opinion. We say the *word is not the thing,* but we know that people react to a notion on the basis of the term that is used to describe it. If we are able to change the name of a band of mercenaries to *freedom fighters,* we are more likely to get financial support from Congress. And if a nuclear missile is unpopular because it is viewed as an offensive weapon, we may be able to create a more favorable impression by giving it a name such as the *Peacekeeper.*

Euphemisms   Discussing subjects that arouse strong emotional feelings often makes us uncomfortable, and we have a tendency to try to soften the impact that abrasive words create. This generally happens when we are talking about something that we fear, such as death, or something that embarrasses us, such as sex. When we use an inoffensive term to conceal our emotional anxiety or embarrassment, we are speaking in euphemisms. For example, we don't like to say that a person died, so we say he "passed away." If we are too embarrassed to say that two unmarried people were having sex, we say they were "having an affair." Euphemisms such as these are generally regarded as proper because they are more polite and less offensive to the senses than the more coarsely worded terminology, but there are others which are designed specifically to avoid confronting the real issue. During the Persian Gulf war when bombs hit a nonmilitary installation and civilians were killed, the press reports would say that there had been "collateral damage," and if our army invaded another country, they would say there had been an "incursion." Language of this kind is defended by the press and by the military on the grounds that it communicates the message in a diplomatic way, but it is criticized by those who say it insulates the listener and the reader from understanding the harsh reality of the event. As a speaker, you will have to make your own judgment on what you believe to be appropriate word usage in a given situation. As a member of the audience, learn to recognize euphemisms so that you will know what is really being said.

Short Cuts   You and your close friends probably have little difficulty in understanding each other. That's because you have developed a conventional meaning for the words that you use which makes it possible for you to take short cuts. You might say to your friend, "You should have come to the party; *everyone* was there." Your meaning of the word *everyone* is, of course, restricted to the people you both know. To clarify your comment for the benefit of someone who didn't understand what you meant, you would have to add specific information to make the abstract meaning more concrete. For example, you would have to say that by the term *everyone* you meant all the students in your speech class, or possibly you would begin to relate the names of some of the people.

Short cuts are often taken intentionally when people don't want to go into detail. Two heads of state, for example, might get together for a top-level conference to discuss differences in their foreign policies. Afterward they may give a statement to the press saying that the talks were "useful."

In that context the term *useful* means they don't want to tell the public any details, but while they didn't come to an agreement, at least they are not at the point of declaring war.

Legal Language   In legal matters it is often necessary to clarify vague terminology in order to translate abstract concepts into principles of law. This is particularly well illustrated in decisions the Supreme Court has made pertaining to the word *speech* as it appears in the First Amendment to the Constitution. Is the meaning of *speech* confined to verbal expression? No, says the Supreme Court. Speech can include certain forms of nonverbal communication; therefore, wearing a black armband as a protest gesture is protected under the First Amendment and is referred to as "symbolic speech." That term was used again in 1989 when the Supreme Court handed down a decision that said the burning of the American flag was also regarded as symbolic speech. If it had been deemed an "act of violence," it could have been prohibited, but since it was construed as a political statement, a legal statute could not forbid it. Each court decision contributes to the legal definition of words, and because law is based on precedence, the terminology from one ruling can be used to clarify our understanding in future cases.

A significant part of being an effective communicator is understanding the conventional meaning society attaches to abstract words. Certainly there is a difference between art that is labeled "erotic" and that which is labeled "pornographic." You might be inclined to say that the difference is only in the mind of the beholder, but that's not good enough when it comes to establishing public policy. Your community may want to place restrictions on one but not on the other, so the language used in verbal descriptions that become codified into law makes a big difference to merchants and patrons of the arts.

Intentional Choice of Words

Choosing words to create a desired impression is in itself an art, and no one knows this better than people in the world of merchandising. Advertising copywriters are paid big salaries for thinking of words that trigger positive responses. Exhaustive studies are conducted to discover the effect certain words have on the public. Terms such as *all new* and *patented formula* are catch phrases specifically designed to make us want to buy the product. Is this practice limited to advertising agencies? By no means—we all do it to one degree or another. If we are *intentional* in our communication, we choose words that generate the kind of feeling we want to evoke in the mind of the receiver of our message.

Certainly there is the question of ethics that we must consider if we are serious students of public speaking and are concerned about taking responsibility for what we say; that is an issue that will be discussed later in the text. Keep in mind that when you are standing on the podium, you have a responsibility to your audience; you are there because you believe you have something to say that will be beneficial to them. If you use words deceptively to create a false impression, you are engaging in sophistry and are violating the traditions of public address.

THE SPEAKER-AUDIENCE RELATIONSHIP

Public address is not an adversarial relationship between the speaker and the audience; it is a cooperative arrangement. Just as there are responsibilities on the part of the person at the podium, so are there common courtesies that should be observed by the people in the audience. The speaker should be able to anticipate that those addressed will be attentive and not obstruct delivery of the message. As we study public speaking, we should also be developing our listening skills, because we know that as

Public address is a cooperative arrangement between the speaker and the audience.

members of the audience we can either enhance or jeopardize the success of the speech. Nothing productive is ever accomplished by heckling a speaker. I know there are some who will say that heckling has been refined to an artform in Hyde Park and that encouraging it is regarded as an acceptable strategy of debate in the Oxford Union. It is also quite common in the British Parliament; nevertheless, it is a practice that impedes reasoned discourse. If you disagree with what a speaker is saying, wait for your turn before you advance your refutation. Heckling is a form of censorship, and all too frequently it silences the views of those who are less aggressive and suppresses ideas that may need to be heard.

The question period that comes after a presentation is a time when the speaker-audience relationship is clearly illustrated. When you are the one on the podium, you hope that there will be questions; that's the way you find out if the audience has been interested and if they have understood what you have been saying. As a member of the audience, you will want to take advantage of the opportunity to enter your own thoughts and concerns into the dialogue. You may be required to stand when you ask your question, which means that you will have to employ the rhetorical skills of a speaker. Be sure to use enough volume so the whole audience can hear you. As a general rule you want to keep your question short; it is a discourtesy to begin making a speech of your own from the floor.

Your job as a speaker is to make your message clear even if you know that what you have to say is controversial and may draw criticism from the audience. If you use language that is intentionally obscure, and you jeopardize the trust relationship that a speaker must have with the audience, you violate your ethical contract. Sometimes we use the term *hidden agenda* to refer to a covert motive that a speaker may have. Assume, for example, that an accountant of a business firm is speaking to a group of its investors. The company has had a series of financial setbacks and is on the verge of bankruptcy; the management does not want the investors to know that. Instead of making a clearly articulated presentation, the accountant deliberately speaks in abstract language, using technical jargon that no one in the audience understands. The hidden agenda in this case is to go through the motions of providing an explanation but to conceal the real information from the listeners. Political figures sometimes find themselves in hot water when a story breaks that suggests there has been an indiscretion or scandal of some kind. This is when a spokesperson who is skillful at handling the press is brought in to minimize the criticism and keep the story from doing too much damage to the politician's image or cause. The procedure is called "damage control," and it refers to the practice of answering questions in such a way as to give as little information as possible and to justify the role that the politician played in the incident.

THE OPPORTUNITY TO BE HEARD

In our Constitution the First Amendment guarantees our right to freedom of speech. This is a privilege that we are inclined to take for granted in the United States because it seems reasonably certain that the amendment will never be repealed. Indeed, the greatest danger to our freedom is more likely to be public apathy than government intervention. We could lose our right to free speech in a very real sense by not exercising it. If we become content to have others speak for us and to allow the positions and interests of the few to dominate public policy and law, we might just as well not have it at all. An important dimension of the First Amendment is that we have the right to *listen,* if we will, and to evaluate what we hear. The consequence of *free speech* is that we will be exposed to all kinds of viewpoints. We will hear false information as well as truth, and we must learn to separate one from the other. That is not always easy and requires that we keep informed on significant issues. Truth is never self-evident; if it were, there would be no need for us to study the art of persuasion. Our Constitution can guarantee that we have the right to speak our minds, but it cannot guarantee that anyone will listen. While what we say may be true, there is no assurance that it will be accepted and believed. If we want to have influence over other people, our government officials, and those who control our institutions, we must be able to make our perception of the truth sound plausible. This ability comes more easily to some than to others, but the opportunity is available to all, regardless of sex, religion, race, nationality, or economic status. It is denied only to those who choose to remain silent.

THE LEGACY OF PUBLIC ADDRESS

Much of the history of the world can be told in the words of orators who spawned or guided significant social, political, and religious movements. The causes that were advocated have not always been beneficial to humanity or civilization; nevertheless, we have all been profoundly influenced by them:

431 B.C.: Pericles, presiding over Greece during the Golden Age, delivered his eulogy called the "Funeral Oration" for the men who had died in battle during the Peloponnesian War. Under his leadership the Greek culture became the inspiration for western civilization.

399 B.C.: Socrates defended his principles and answered charges of "corrupting the youth" to the Council of Five Hundred in his speech of defense called "The Apology." Though he was critical of the sophists who taught the art of persuasion, he himself spoke eloquently.

44 B.C.: Marc Antony faced a hostile audience after the assassination of

Julius Caesar, but he reversed the sentiments of the people with oratory that "raised the stones of Rome" as he called for mutiny against Brutus.

1521: Martin Luther, after a series of disputes with the pope, appeared before Charles V at Worms and said, "Here I stand; I can do no other." His defiance of the Catholic church resulted in the Reformation and the rise of the Protestant movement.

1775: Patrick Henry delivered his fiery address at St. John's Church in Richmond, Virginia, during the revolutionary convention. His words rallied the colonial militia to confront the British forces at Lexington and Concord, signaling the start of the American Revolution.

1863: Abraham Lincoln spoke only briefly at the dedication ceremony in Gettysburg, Pennsylvania, but his words brought hope to a nation in the midst of a devastating Civil War. As Pericles had done, he honored the soldiers who had fallen on both sides during the battle.

1925: Clarence Darrow achieved his reputation for courtroom speaking with his defense of union organizer Eugene Debs. In a later trial he debated the famous orator and prosecuting attorney William Jennings Bryan when charges were brought against John Scopes for teaching the theory of evolution in public schools. Darrow lost the case but won the cause.

1932: Adolf Hitler used the beer halls of Munich as his speaking forum and projected the Nazi party into power with his tirades against the Jews and the Bolsheviks. His flamboyant oratorical style is credited with the success of the movement.

1940: Winston Churchill gave hope and inspiration to the British people after the retreat from Dunkirk and assured them victory over the German war machine, even though he could offer nothing more than "blood, sweat, and tears."

1963: Martin Luther King spoke of his dream from the steps of the Lincoln Memorial to a crowd of over 200,000 people. He raised the consciousness of the nation for the cause of racial equality and set the wheels in motion for civil rights legislation and freedom from discrimination.

1988: Mikhail Gorbachev described a "new world order" for the twenty-first century in his speech to the United Nations. He defused the threat of military force as an instrument of foreign policy, introduced the terms *glasnost* and *perestroika* to the lexicon of political language, and presided over the tearing down of the Berlin Wall and the restructuring of the Soviet Union.

The list could be extended much further. From this country alone we could add the names of Franklin Roosevelt, Wendell Willkie, and John F. Kennedy—all of whom used the spoken word to influence thought and effect social changes. As students of public address, we need to recognize and appreciate the power that emanates from the speaker's podium.

Martin Luther King raised the consciousness of the nation for the cause of racial equality.

As well as promoting causes, oratorical skills also advance the position of the speaker. In the summer of 1988 during the presidential campaign, the Republican candidate trailed the Democratic contender by 12 percentage points in most of the nationwide public opinion surveys. On the day after George Bush delivered his acceptance speech at the Republican convention, the situation reversed, and Bush was leading Michael Dukakis by 12 points. Whatever your political persuasion, you have to consider that to be one very successful speech.

The Historical Perspective

As far back as 2080 B.C. an aging pharaoh gave some advice to his son, Merykare, who would succeed him: "Be a craftsman in speech (so that) you mayest be strong. . . . The tongue is a sword . . . and speech is more valorous than fighting."[3]

The words had little practical application for the rank and file of his subjects, however, since the pharaoh was not a man who tolerated members of the general population making speeches in the public square. It was, in fact, another 1600 years before there appeared a social climate conducive to the study of public speaking. The first noteworthy scholar of the art was the Greek philosopher Corax, who began writing and teaching in about 480 B.C. At that time the Greek city-states were experimenting

---

[3] "Elba, Splendor of an Unknown Empire," *National Geographic,* December 1978, p. 750.

with a democratic form of government—a concept that was completely unheard of before then. There was a legal procedure that permitted people charged with a crime to defend themselves in court. The defendants, however, were not allowed to have an attorney; they had to plead the case themselves. This system created a need for instruction. Those who lacked communication skills sought the services of Corax and others like him to receive coaching in the art of public speaking. Corax originated some of the basic principles that we teach today, including the organizational structure of a speech and the elements of persuasion. He laid the groundwork for the scholars who were to follow—Socrates, Plato, and the most important contributor, Aristotle.

THE ART OF RHETORIC

Traditionally the speaker's art is referred to as rhetoric, and it was Aristotle who provided us with the best definition. He said, "Let rhetoric be defined as an ability, in each particular case to see the *available means of persuasion*. . . . This is the function of no other art, for each of the others is instructive and persuasive about its own subject. . . ."[4] In other words the study of *how* to explain and persuade has subject matter of its own which is separate from the body of knowledge that is central to any particular discipline. It is for this reason that public speaking is taught as an individual subject.

The "available means of persuasion" refers primarily to the power of words to create mental images, to provide explanations, to introduce concepts, to organize ideas, and to offer supporting evidence. In the context of public speaking, the "available means of persuasion" also refers to vocal inflection, gesticulation, and every other aspect of oral delivery. Because there are so many variables, the best way to study rhetoric is to observe those who apply the art in an effective manner and to analyze what they are doing. This is precisely what Aristotle did and, subsequently, what other scholars have done in studying the art of rhetoric.

Aristotle's definition suggests that rhetoric is an applied art. It can add a practical dimension to your academic pursuits because it will help you put to use the information you learn in other subject areas. In applying the art of rhetoric, you have an opportunity to pull together the principles inherent in the arts, humanities, and sciences so that you can see the relationships and how the ideas are interconnected. In the process of learning how to express what you know and how to influence other people, you will find that your education will begin to take on new significance.

Contemporary thought has contributed a great deal to the study of oral

---

[4] Aristotle, *On Rhetoric,* George A. Kennedy (trans.), Oxford University Press, New York, 1991, pp. 36–37.

communication, but the principles of rhetoric outlined by Aristotle in 336 B.C. provide the basis for just about everything that has been written on the subject since that time. A great many college textbooks, including this one, borrow heavily from his fundamental model of the audience, the message, and the speaker.

The Audience

The communication process does not begin until you have an audience—someone to receive the message that you send. You probably would not bother to talk in an empty room unless you were practicing your delivery. Only when someone else is present do we have the *potential* for communication, and even then we know that it might not occur unless the person is listening and has some capacity for understanding. Often speakers believe that what they mean to say is replicated in the listener's mind, but that is not always the case. You need to be realistic about your ability to communicate and understand that the *message is the message received.* What you intend your message to be is the way it is for you, but the message *received* is the way it is for the listener.

The Message

When people take courses in public speaking, they often feel that the most difficult part will be conquering their fears of facing an audience and learning the skills of delivery. While those two elements may initially be the significant concerns of a student, the most important consideration in speechmaking is the quality of the message. As students begin to understand what public address is all about, they learn that the most difficult part is gathering the information and putting it together in a well-organized fashion.

Content   In classical rhetoric the process of developing the content of the speech is called the *inventio*. In contemporary language you could say it's preparing the *substance*. This is the time when you examine your resources to discover what information you want to include in the message. What you say should be something that you, yourself, have found to be interesting and significant, but most important it must be a message that will be useful in some way to the audience. The best source of material for a speech is the information that is already in your head, but you may have to embellish that with ideas and evidence that you gather from your research. Take as much time as you need in the planning stage. Don't be motivated by what is the easiest thing to say, but instead think in terms of what will be of the greatest value to the audience.

Structure   As we have observed, public speaking is a structured form of communication—the progression of ideas forms a pattern and moves in a logical sequence from the beginning to the end. That characteristic may not be prevalent in other forms of oral communication. In ordinary conversation, for example, we may ramble, go off on tangents, and perhaps never reach any kind of conclusion. We don't prepare for conversations as we prepare for speeches; consequently, they may contain a limited amount of factual information, cumbersome expression of ideas, and many digressions to trivialities. The intent here is not to be critical of conversation, but rather to point out how it differs from public speaking. The advantage in prepared and structured communication is that it is a faster and more readily comprehensible means of transmitting the message to the listener. Conversation can be fun and often informative, but it is very time-consuming. Class discussion can also be stimulating and enjoyable, but for the sake of efficiency, a professor can cover more material in a shorter period of time by delivering a well-prepared lecture.

The Speaker

Seeking opportunities to speak in public may not be something that occupies a great deal of your time. However, even without looking for them, you will find that such occasions occur frequently, and they present you with a chance to give expression to beliefs or experiences you would like to share. Some occasions at which you could speak might be a graduation ceremony, a business meeting, a memorial service, or a town-hall gathering. The setting could be in a school, a church, a home, a conference room, or an auditorium. One excellent opportunity for developing proficiency in public speaking is to become a member of Toastmasters International. You probably will be able to find a local chapter by looking in your telephone directory.

But why would a person volunteer to give a speech in the first place? Sitting in the audience is much more comfortable than standing on a speaker's platform. What is it that causes people to accept the risk of criticism and rejection for the sake of having their ideas expressed in a public forum? Do these people suffer less from speech fright? Not necessarily. They probably have the same anxieties as everyone else. Are they people who are smarter or better informed than others? Maybe, but maybe not. You might know just as much as they do. The difference is that they are *willing* to do it.

Willingness is an important factor in the process of developing public speaking skills. In order to make any progress at all, you must be able to set aside negative attitudes you might have and convince yourself that there is real value in the effort you will be called upon to expend. Your willingness to speak may develop as a result of your perception that something needs to be said; however, that might not be sufficient motivation for you if you perceive the risk to be greater than the reward. What do you have to gain from exposing your ideas to the scrutiny of an audience?

1 You have a chance to clarify your thinking and gain a firmer grasp on what you believe by organizing your ideas in a way that makes them understandable for you and for others.

2 You may succeed in motivating other people to support a cause that is important to you.

3 You demonstrate leadership capabilities and show others that you are able and willing to take responsibility.

4 You build your self-confidence and raise your self-esteem by learning to defend the positions that you take on controversial issues.

5 You enrich your life with new relationships by attracting people who share your interests and points of view.

There is, perhaps, one more personal value connected to the study of public speaking skills, and that is an appreciation for rational thought. The student who takes the art seriously becomes part of a tradition that goes back thousands of years. Aristotle said, "It is absurd to hold that a man ought to be ashamed of being unable to defend himself with his limbs, but not of being unable to defend himself with speech and reason, when the use of rational speech is more distinctive of a human being than the use of his limbs."[5]

In a society that seems to value physical prowess over effective articulation, we may wonder how much impact Aristotle's assertion has had. It is unlikely that a debate tournament will ever draw as many spectators as a football game. Yet, it is certainly true that in a civilized culture, we rely more heavily on our verbal abilities than on our physical strength to defend our lives, our property, and our principles.

GETTING STARTED

There is much to learn about the preparation and delivery of a good speech. As you proceed in the reading of this text, you will get some insight into the basic theory, and as you begin to give speeches in class, you will discover that experience is the best teacher. Here is a brief checklist of what you need to know to get started.

---

[5] Ibid.

1 Content. Your first step is to pick a topic that meets the assignment you are given. Choose one that interests you and contains examples the audience will find significant and relevant. Start by thinking of topics about which you already have some knowledge or familiarity.

2 Organization. The information must be arranged in some sort of logical sequence, so plan on making an outline. Give thought to your organizational structure, and stick to that pattern when you present the material. Make sure you have a statement of purpose, clearly phrased main contentions, specific information that is relevant to your main ideas, and a conclusion to reinforce what you have said.

3 Language. Don't write the speech out word for word; plan on delivering it extemporaneously from your outline. When you speak, choose language that effectively communicates your meaning, pronounce words correctly, and use proper and appropriate grammar.

4 Voice. Use enough volume so that you can be heard by everyone in the room, and enunciate your words and syllables clearly. Employ vocal inflection to place emphasis on key words and phrases.

5 Timing and pacing. Be sure to start and end the speech on time. Speak fast enough to keep your audience awake and to have time to cover all your material, but not so rapidly that you run words together.

6 Attitude. Before you begin to give the speech, develop a positive attitude toward the subject matter and toward the audience. Convey a sense of interest and enthusiasm for what you are saying and let the audience know that you think it's important for them to listen.

7 Appearance. Project an air of confidence to the audience; stand up straight and maintain eye contact with your listeners. Your posture, gestures, and facial expressions should reinforce the message. Be sure to dress appropriately for the occasion.

8 Integrity. Honesty and sincerity are the hallmarks of effective public speaking. Never attempt to deceive an audience or exploit them in any way. Maintain a high ethical standard for your own sake as well as for theirs.

These are the criteria that will probably be used when you give your speeches in class. Your fellow students in the audience may make observations about what they saw and heard, and, of course, your instructor will give you a grade. But rather than relying entirely on the feedback you get from other people, learn to be your own critic. Keep these criteria in mind as you prepare your speech and as you deliver it, and afterward make your own evaluation of how well you did. Try to discover for yourself what worked and what didn't work, and never let an opportunity go by without learning something from the experience.

EXERCISE

Under the heading "The Legacy of Public Address" there are names of several famous people who affected the world in a powerful way through the application of their oratorical skills. Select one name, read about what the person did, and make a brief report to the class. Use the following framework as your organizational structure.

- Start by telling the person's name, title, nationality, and period in history.
- Describe briefly the significant social conditions that prevailed in the person's time.
- Relate the point of view expressed in one or more of the person's speeches.
- Quote at least one line of what the person said.
- Conclude with the results that were achieved by the person's oratorical efforts.

QUESTIONS FOR REVIEW

1 What are the three essential elements in any model of communication?

2 What do we mean when we say communication is "transactional"?

3 What is the difference between structured and unstructured communication?

4 How does communication in a committee or a task force differ from ordinary conversation?

5 What is meant by *impromptu* speaking?

6 What are the features that distinguish the public speaking model of communication from those that are less structured?

7 What is meant by the term *noise*? How does physical noise differ from psychological noise?

8 How do you define the study of semantics?

9 What do we mean by *icons*? How do they differ from other pictorial art?

10 What is meant by *operational meaning*?

11 How do words at the high end of the scale of abstraction differ from those at the low end?

12 What do we mean by *semantic reactions*? Give examples.

13 What did the Supreme Court mean by the term *symbolic speech*?

14 What is meant by the term *sophistry*?

15 What is meant by *hidden agenda*?

16 How did Aristotle define the word *rhetoric*?

PREPARING TO MEET THE AUDIENCE

The more you know about the people to whom you are speaking, the better prepared you will be to adapt your presentation to their needs. Giving a talk to a group of your friends or to members of an organization with which you are affiliated simplifies the task of planning what you need to say. You would have some understanding of how much they already know about the topic and how much technical detail you could include. You would also have a certain amount of insight into their feelings and attitudes toward the subject matter that you plan to cover. If some part of your presentation is controversial, you would know when and where you might expect to encounter opposition. But when you are speaking to a group of strangers, your task is more difficult. Suppose you receive an invitation from the program chairperson of a local service club to speak at its weekly luncheon meeting—what do you do?

LOGISTICS

You need to find out what you can about the logistics of the speaking occasion—the date and the time (make sure you note that information on your calendar), the size of the group, the way the seating will be arranged, and whether or not you will need a public-address system. Certainly, you want to know how long you are expected to speak and if there is to be a question period afterward. You should know if there are going to be other speakers on the program and, if so, what their topics will be. If you plan to

25

use visual aids, find out what facilities are available. You may need an easel for charts, a chalkboard, or perhaps a projector and screen. These things are not generally provided unless you request them—even if you are a prominent person. When Queen Elizabeth II was invited to speak at the White House, for example, she may have assumed that all provisions would be made for her. Unfortunately, no one thought about her need to stand on a raised platform. She gave what may have been an excellent speech, but all that anyone was able to see of her over the lectern was the top of her hat. So try to anticipate what your particular needs might be.

DEMOGRAPHICS

Next, find out from the person who invited you as much as you can about the *demographics* of the audience—that means their age, sex, vocation, socioeconomic status, education, religion, politics, ethnic background, and anything else that might affect their beliefs, attitudes, and perceptions. That information does not have to be scientifically gathered; it can be based simply on casual observations made by someone who is familiar with those to whom you will be speaking. People frequently use demographic analysis to assess groups in many everyday situations, whether they realize it or not, so it may be that all you have to do is inquire.[1] Knowing just a few specific characteristics about your audience will help you plan a speech that is relevant to their needs and interests. The people who serve as program directors for large organizations that invite speakers on a regular basis often distribute questionnaires to their audiences to collect demographic information that they can use for planning purposes. Be sure to ask if such a survey has been taken and if the results would be available to you.

ADAPTING YOUR SPEECH TO THE AUDIENCE

Let's say, for example, that you have been invited to speak to the Junior Chamber of Commerce in your community. You can probably expect an audience of men and women in their late twenties and early thirties who are college-educated and career-oriented. Their affiliation with the Jaycees tells you that they probably have a concern for social issues, particularly those that affect the local economy. Knowing this about them makes it possible for you to select examples that are within their frame of reference. That's easier to do when you are in the same age bracket, but

---

[1] C. William Colburn and Sanford B. Weinber, "An Orientation to Listening and Audience Analysis," *Modcom: Modules in Speech Communication*, Science Research Associates, Chicago, 1976, p. 24.

an older speaker (such as me) has to bear in mind that references to social conditions which existed "before the war" (in reference to World War II) do not clearly communicate to a generation born thirty years later. They will want to know which war. Certainly I can talk about the depression years of the 1930s, but I must remember that my audience did not live through them. As a young person talking to an audience of senior citizens, you have a similar problem. Terminology that you use all the time may have a different meaning to people thirty years older than yourself. If you are speaking on leisure time activities and suggest they buy a CD, they might be thinking "certificate of deposit" when you mean "compact disc." Even though your topic is one that might appeal to any generation, the references and examples you use might be different for one group than they would be for another.

Consider Particular Interests

Suppose you have been asked to speak because of your association with the local college or university. That gives you some idea of what interest the audience has, but the subject area is still pretty broad. You want to address the concerns of your audience, so you need still more information about them. It may be that you have been invited so that a group of high school students can hear you. In this case you would orient your remarks to those who are considering enrollment in the college. You could talk about the courses that are offered, scholarships and financial aid, social activities, athletics, and other aspects of college life that would be of interest to incoming students. What if you were addressing the business executives of the community—the ones who pay the taxes that support the college? Here your approach would be quite different. You might discuss the funding of programs, the financial health of the institution, the research that is being done that will benefit business and industry, and the cultural offerings. If your audience were made up of graduate students and prospective teachers, you might talk about academic freedom in the classroom, the quality of education, or the role that the faculty plays in the governance of the college. These are just three examples of entirely different speeches in the same subject area, each designed for the interest of a specific audience.

In terms of the subject matter itself, I believe you can adapt just about any topic to suit the interest and the understanding of the audience. The people in the Junior Chamber of Commerce, for example, would probably be just as concerned about Social Security as members of the American Association of Retired Persons. The difference might be that the Jaycees would want to know about new taxation laws, and the members of AARP would be more interested in benefits. But that's just a difference in your emphasis. One word of caution: Be very careful about making generalized assumptions based on conventional stereotypes. Older people are not always conservative, and young folks are not necessarily progressive; a great many women have an interest in science, and there are a lot of men who enjoy cooking. Avoid the mistake of allowing people in the audience to believe that you have classified them into restricted categories.

Recognize Possible Opposition

Try to understand the particular orientation of the audience you plan to address, and make an informed guess as to how willing they will be to accept your message. This advice does not imply that you must always try to appease your listeners; there will be times when you may have to say things they don't want to hear. In one of his campaign speeches, Robert Kennedy made the statement on a university campus that he did not believe that students should be exempt from the draft. The crowd booed and Kennedy reminded them that they had said he should "tell it like it is." By analyzing the audience's perspective you may be able to think of ways to penetrate their defenses and phrase the controversial statement in words they are willing to consider. You may not be able to anticipate all possible objections, but you should be ready for the obvious ones. If you are giving a speech to members of the American Bar Association as Vice President Dan Quayle did in August of 1991, and you blame the legal profession for a "self-inflicted competitive disadvantage" to the nation's economy by allowing the country to have 70 percent of the world's lawyers and 18 million new lawsuits a year, you can be sure that your remarks will invite rebuttal. Certainly you have a right to say that, and the criticism might even be justified, but don't be surprised by the reaction. Be sure you are armed with strong evidence and have a game plan for responding to the objections.

THE AUDIENCE IS PLURAL

The word *audience* is a term that can be used to refer to one person or to many. Normally we think of an audience as a gathering of people listening to one or more speakers, but the grammar of our language tends to distort the meaning. *Audience* is a collective noun and is commonly used with a singular verb—we say, "The audience is . . ." The implication here is that the listeners will respond as one person, but we know that such is not the case. We may tend to believe that an all-male audience will like a speech on sports and will be able to understand our references, but in reality we are making a generalization that is going to have some exceptions. Each individual in the audience has a different level of comprehension, and each will be affected by our message in a different way.

Each person in the audience is the final arbiter of what is believed, what is held to be true, and what is thought to be right.

Even those men in the audience who are interested in sports and do understand your references may perceive your message in a way that is different from what you intended. Each will be receiving what he regards as important, rejecting that which is unacceptable, disregarding what is not comprehensible, and perhaps even modifying some of your most cherished notions. Regardless of how disturbing this observation might be, it is necessary for us to understand that the audience is the final arbiter of what is believed, what is held to be true, and what is thought to be right.[2] People are going to listen only to what they are willing to hear.

Public speaking has a significant disadvantage relative to conversational communication. In conversation you can make one point at a time and get a reaction to it before you go on to the next one, but this procedure would encumber the public speaking mode by taking too much time and by diverting the speaker away from a planned organizational pattern. Public speakers using good organization and effective techniques can communicate a large amount of information to a great many people in a

[2] Joseph A. DeVito, *Elements of Public Speaking,* 2d ed., Harper & Row, New York, 1984, p. 106.

short period of time, but they may not know until after the speech is over whether or not the listeners understood and accepted what was said.

CULTURAL DIVERSITY

The most important audience analysis you do is that which pertains to the characteristics of the actual group you will be addressing, but you can get some understanding of the broad picture by examining demographics at the national and regional levels. *Time* magazine reports that the growing number of Asians, blacks, and Hispanics will mean that the white population in the United States will be in the minority by the twenty-first century.[3] The report goes on to say that right now 40 percent of elementary and secondary school children in New York belong to an ethnic minority, and in California, Asian, black, and Hispanic students already outnumber Caucasians. These statistics say nothing, of course, about the cultural makeup of a specific audience, but they do suggest that there is a good chance your listeners will not all have the same ethnic background.

Given the fact that we are a culturally diverse nation, what kind of assumptions can a speaker make about the probable reactions of a general audience, particularly when the topic of the speech deals with social issues? "Rather than accepting U.S. history and its meaning as settled, citizens will feel ever more free to debate where the nation's successes sprang from and what its unalterable beliefs are. They will clash over which myths and icons to invoke in education, in popular culture, and in ceremonial speechmaking from political campaigns to the State of the Union Address."[4] Developing insight into how people might react to the speeches you give has broader implications than just those that pertain to the study of oral communication; it will help you get along better with people on a day-to-day basis. The attitude that members of the audience have toward events in American history such as the winning of the west, the defense of the Alamo, and the use of Chinese labor for building of the railroads may vary depending on their individual ethnic origins. As a speaker you need to recognize that the perspective you have is not necessarily going to be shared by all the members of your audience.

Social and Economic Differences

Failure to communicate effectively from the podium may occur when the audience believes that the speaker does not understand or does not appre-

---

[3] William A. Henry, III, "Beyond the Melting Pot," *Time,* Apr. 9, 1990, pp. 28–29.
[4] Ibid.

ciate the values and the attitudes of those who are being addressed. Cultural differences may sometimes interfere with your ability to gain the respect of the audience if you are perceived as a person whose perspective on life is significantly different from theirs. If you were reared in a middle-class neighborhood, it may be difficult for you to relate to the experience of people who were brought up in a minority ghetto. There is much to be gained in a college classroom when there is some measure of cultural diversity—particularly in a speech class where students have the opportunity to share their experiences and talk about their beliefs, attitudes, values, and feelings. One subject area that is frequently discussed is that of social welfare. Opposition to such programs as subsidized housing generally comes from people who have spent their entire lives in middle-class suburban neighborhoods and have never known anyone who was living on welfare. For the most part, attitudes are formed by mental pictures of welfare recipients as lazy, irresponsible, and probably dishonest. That's when it can be beneficial to have someone in the class who is able to dispel the image by revealing that he or she was reared in a subsidized housing unit by a parent receiving welfare. The effect is better still when the person who has had that experience is intelligent and articulate and can testify to the critical support that social welfare programs can provide. One of the important contributions to education afforded by the study of public speaking is that it fosters the development of a broad perspective on life. People who are the most effective speakers are those who are able to recognize that the point of view they are expressing is not the only one that exists. Speakers who do not learn this are going to be confronted by questions they did not anticipate coming out of attitudes they never considered.

Changes in Attitudes and Beliefs

Factors that affect changes in attitudes and beliefs have been examined extensively. One study conducted at Ohio State University concluded that personal relevance, argumentative strength, and source credibility were the three most important elements in determining whether or not a belief structure would be modified.[5] A high personal relevance factor means that an individual has a lot to gain or to lose if a particular course of action is followed. For example, someone who is employed in an industry that depends on government contracts for military aircraft will probably be very much opposed to making cuts in defense spending. You, on the

---

[5] Richard Petty and John Cacioppo, *Attitudes and Persuasion: Classic and Contemporary Approaches,* Brown, Dubuque, Iowa, 1981.

other hand, may believe that world peace is jeopardized when vast numbers of weapons are produced. The person employed in the defense industry is going to be very difficult to convince and may not be moved by abstract arguments based solely on humanitarian concepts of justice and human rights. The promotion of world peace may be very important to you, but the recipient of the message will be thinking about the possibility of being laid off and how he or she is going to pay the bills and support the family if there is no income.

When the personal relevance factor is high, strong argumentation is needed that will satisfy the concerns of the message receivers. You would have to be able to convince defense workers that they would not lose their jobs, or that new and perhaps better employment could be found after the industry was converted to manufacturing a peacetime product. On the other hand, specifically tailored argumentation may not be necessary when the personal relevance factor is low. If your audience is composed of people who have secure jobs in non-military-related industries, there is not much risk for them. Under those circumstances they may be willing to take what the researchers at Ohio State University called the "peripheral route" and accept your point of view on the basis of source credibility. That means if they can accept your thesis without having their lives severely affected, and if they like you and believe you can be trusted, they may go along with your point of view without requiring that you give a lot of supporting evidence.

Anticipating Reaction

Trying to analyze how listeners might react toward a point of view you want to express on a complex issue is not an easy task. Even if you ask people how they feel, you can't always be sure that your interpretation of their answers will be accurate, because they may not have it completely sorted out in their own minds. During the Persian Gulf crisis polltakers asked a great many people, "Do you support a military invasion of Iraq?" It is difficult to give a simple yes or no answer to a question like that. A thinking person might want to say, "I regret that our diplomatic and intelligence efforts were not successful in anticipating the crisis so that we found ourselves in a position that made war the only option. I might be willing to support a military invasion provided that it have the endorsement of the United Nations and the approval of the U.S. Congress; I would want some assurance that every effort would be made to protect the lives of civilian populations, and I would want to know what the goals would be of such an operation." What does that all add up to? Yes or no? The point is that complex issues are never black and white, and if you believe that they are, you might not recognize support for your position that comes from people who may basically agree with you but find it necessary to qualify their response.

POLITICAL PERSPECTIVES

A good way to get experience in audience analysis is to work as a volunteer for a political candidate. You will develop an understanding of the extent to which politicians go to discover the best approaches to gain the voters' attention and favor. Large political organizations at the national level try to hone their techniques to a science by compiling massive amounts of data that reveal the particular issues of concern to every demographic profile in each section of the country. Speeches that are given by politicians and their supporters can then be tailored to fit a specific audience.

In recent years it has become increasingly difficult to predict the voting patterns of the American people. For one reason, there are a great many independent voters who do not align themselves with any particular political party. And even those who do choose a party often do not feel a sense of loyalty to it. There was a time when you could be fairly certain which side of a controversial issue would be taken by people who described themselves as Democrats or Republicans, and you could discover what they believed by reading the platforms that were drawn up by the party leaders. But election analysts have a much more difficult time now because candidates themselves do not always agree with what is written into their own party's platform. Also there are a great many people who have become "single-issue voters." This is a term that applies to people who will vote for a candidate only if he or she has taken the "correct" stand on one particular issue. It may have to do with capital punishment, gun control, abortion, or taxes—but whatever it is, the single-issue voter will disregard all other matters or personal characteristics and focus only on that one item.

Taxation is always an important issue in elections, but since the early 1980s it has been particularly crucial. Presidential and gubernatorial candidates find themselves in a real dilemma because the public needs government services that require revenue, but a great many people won't vote for politicians who say they will increase taxes. This political fact cost Walter Mondale the election in 1984, and no candidate since then has wanted to make the same mistake.

If you are giving a speech in support of a political candidate, your best strategy would be to describe the accomplishments and the qualifications of the person rather than attempt to interpret his or her policies. Surveys have indicated that people often decide to vote for someone on the basis of personal characteristics that they like, even though they disagree with the candidate on policy matters. Ronald Reagan became one of the country's most popular presidents because he was regarded as a "great communicator," even though the people who voted for him often disagreed with the stands he took on specific issues. If we perceive that candidates seem to be putting a lot of emphasis upon "image," it's because they know that the persona they project may have more to do with their getting elected than their foreign or domestic policies.

Descriptive Labels

Analyzing expected audience reaction is uncertain even when you have access to demographic information, because over the years labels that have been used to describe political inclinations have become blurred. You might be able to make broad generalizations about groups that are said to be "conservative" or "liberal," but these categories are unreliable when it comes to making predictions regarding the way individual audience members will respond. Contrary to what you might think, there are conservatives who favor the legalization of marijuana and liberals who vote to increase military spending. Given this, how can you as a speaker predict audience reaction even when you know that your listeners are Republican or Democrat, or that they favor a conservative or liberal point of view? The answer is that regardless of who your audience may be, the presentation you make must be reasonable and supportable. If it is, even those who disagree will be obliged to respect your position. When you are speaking on a controversial issue, you never want to assume that you will have 100 percent approval. And conversely, it's not a good idea to expect complete disapproval, either; if you do, you may find yourself sounding defensive.

RELIGIOUS AFFILIATIONS

In this country we try to keep politics separated from religion, but that's a little like trying to keep the wind away from the rain. In the presidential campaign of 1960 many people were concerned over the fact that John F. Kennedy was a Roman Catholic. While there had been Catholic candidates before (Al Smith in 1928), none had ever been elected to the top executive office. People feared that a Catholic president would be taking orders from the pope in Rome, or at least that's what Kennedy's opponents said. As it turned out, the election was very close, but analysts have concluded that religion did not play a significant part in the campaign. That election was an important breakthrough in U.S. politics; Catholics now know that their religion does not exclude them from winning a presidential election.

There is no question that religious background is going to have an effect on a person's thinking, but we must realize that our predictions about what a person in public office will do can often be wrong. For example, even though Kennedy was a Catholic, he still opposed supporting parochial schools with public funds. While we tend to identify certain religious persuasions with particular social issues, we need to note that even within a given denomination itself there is going to be disagreement. Students often regard churches as being morally or politically conservative. The fact is that church people are represented on both sides of issues such as abortion, capital punishment, homosexuality, and military intervention, and a great many clergy from all denominations have played a leading role in social reform movements of this century. If you are asked to speak at a church function, you can expect to find the same kind of diversity as you would in any other group of concerned citizens.

HOW WELL DOES AN AUDIENCE LISTEN?

On the average, 70 percent of our waking hours are spent in some form of verbal communication—reading, writing, speaking, or listening; of that amount of time, 42 percent involves listening.[6] With all that practice, you might think that the receptive skills of an audience would be highly developed, but don't count on it. Even though listening is an extremely important skill, not much instruction on it is given in our public schools, because it is very difficult to teach. We know how to teach people to speak—we can provide them with methods and guidelines, let them try it, observe their behavior, and critique their performance. Speaking is an observable art, but listening is not. We can't know for sure if people are listening just by watching their reactions. We can make some guesses based on their facial expressions and eye contact, but nonverbal feedback often proves to be inaccurate. In a classroom, of course, the instructor can give students a quiz to test their comprehension of a lecture, but you do not have that opportunity in an average speaking situation. The fact is that an audience may stop listening without your ever knowing it.

STEPPING INTO THE LISTENERS' SHOES

You can get some insight into the listening habits of the average audience by reflecting on your own listening behavior patterns. You may regard yourself as someone who is able to pay attention to a speaker most of the time, but the chances are that you have the same obstacles to overcome

---

[6] William J. Seiler, E. Scott Baudhuin, and L. David Schuelke, *Communication in Business and Professional Organizations*, Addison-Wesley, Reading, Mass., 1982, p. 136.

that everyone else has. Let's say, for example, that you've had plenty of sleep, the time is mid-morning, the environment is comfortable and attractive, and the topic is one that interests you. Even under those ideal circumstances are you going to be able to hear and retain everything?

- Do you normally start listening from the very beginning of the speech?
- Are you generally able to construct a clear picture of the speaker's main idea?
- Are you able to recognize all the points that are really important, and can you grasp new information as well as that which you have heard before?
- Can you connect the specific information to the generalizations?
- Do you make a practice of giving the speaker your undivided attention without allowing your thoughts to drift away to other matters that concern you?
- Are you able to sustain your attention when a speaker is tedious or hard to hear, or has mannerisms that annoy you?
- Do you never allow prejudices based on age, race, sex, or ethnic origin to get in the way of your hearing a speaker's message?
- Do you listen all the way through to the end to hear how the speaker's conclusion reinforces the main idea of the speech?

If you can answer "yes" to all of those questions, you are truly remarkable. But if your listening habits fall short of being perfect, you can understand that the average person is going to have difficulties as well.

SPEAKING SO PEOPLE WILL LISTEN

Public speaking would be a lot easier if we could select for our audience only those people who are skilled and highly motivated listeners. But, alas, we can't do that. We have to take whatever audience we get and do what we can to gain and hold their attention. The challenge of the speaker is to ease the task of the listeners and overcome whatever obstacles impede the reception of the message. We have a better chance of doing that if we know what those obstacles are.

Gain the Attention

In order to listen effectively, the audience needs to be *ready* to listen, and that readiness may not always coincide with the beginning of the speaker's message. Communication breakdowns often occur at the very start of a presentation if the listener is thinking about something else when the

The challenge of the speaker is to ease the task of the listeners and overcome obstacles that impede reception of the message.

speaker is providing orientation to the message. *Solution:* The speaker must do something or say something that will gain the atten.ion of the audience before launching into the main idea of the message. We call this the *attention statement.* It might consist of a humorous anecdote, a quotation, a rhetorical question, a reference to the occasion, or just a word of welcome, but it is as important to an audience as a starter is to an automobile.

Have a Clear Purpose Statement

If the audience fails to understand your main idea, the thrust of your speech will be lost. People will become confused, frustrated, and perhaps even antagonistic. They should not have to guess at your purpose or position, and they should not have to sort through a maze of obscure language to find it. *Solution:* As soon as you are sure you have gained the attention of the audience, make a clearly phrased statement that provides orientation to the topic and to your point of view. The statement should be sufficiently qualified so that it focuses on what you want to say and excludes any tangential aspects of the topic that you do not plan to cover.

Emphasize Key Words and Important Points

It's easy for people to listen to what they already know; it's much more difficult for them to expand their vocabulary and their fund of knowledge by learning something new. They may find it difficult to perceive the value of a specific piece of information and fail to retain the key words or important points. *Solution:* Identify in your own mind what is important for the audience to remember; then think of ways to emphasize those items. For example, if you are going to use a key word that you think they might be hearing for the first time, you have to say it more than once. *Repetition* is the most effective means you have for facilitating audience retention. You could also *write the word* on a chalkboard or flip-chart; you could use *vocal emphasis*—modulating your pitch or volume. A very easy device to use is a *pointer phrase,* such as "It's important to remember that . . . ," calling attention to the fact that what follows is a significant part of the speech.

Provide Connecting Phrases

It's not just the retention of specific information that is difficult, but also the ability to see connections. The audience needs to understand how the specifics relate to the main idea and how they support the thesis. Here again, the speaker must not rely on listeners' being able to tie everything together by themselves. *Solution:* Help the audience see the significance of the information by using *connecting phrases* to link the data to the generalizations. The listening process is greatly enhanced when speakers use such expressions as "What we can see from this fact is that . . ."

Build Attention Features into the Speech

You may believe that what you want to tell your listeners is the most important thing they need to know; however, there are going to be other matters on their minds. One listener is concerned about the unfavorable evaluation he has just received from his supervisor; another has remembered that he is double-parked, and a third person has just found out that she is pregnant. All these things are on the minds of the people who you believe should primarily be interested in your speech on the possible extinction of the spotted owl. *Solution:* Build into your presentation features of interest that are designed to capture and hold the attention of the audience. These features need to be woven into the speech so that they contribute to the content rather than being interruptions. *Humor* is one of the best features to use—not jokes necessarily, but humorous phrases and references. When you are researching your topic, look for *unusual examples* that will grab the listeners' attention, and try if you can to *tailor the example* to an interest of the audience. Visual aids can also be interest features; more will be said about them in a later chapter.

Ease the Strain of Listening

What we know about listening is that it is not easy, and people who are not highly motivated to pay attention may tune out if they are given an excuse to do so. Certainly it is true that they should not give up on you even if your volume is a bit low or your voice is monotone, but the fact is that they often do. If listening to you becomes too difficult, or if they perceive something about you they don't like, they may conclude that it's not worth the effort, regardless of how important the message may be. *Solution:* Don't give the audience a reason to stop listening. Speak loud enough and clearly enough so that you can be heard, and modulate your voice so you are not talking in a monotone. Dress appropriately for the occasion. Learn what behavior characteristics are distracting to an audience and make an effort to avoid them. Don't try to put on airs by bragging and showing off your knowledge, and don't "talk down" to people as though they were inferior to you.

Penetrate Stereotyped Notions

People in the audience should not reject the message because of stereotypes they have formed about the race, nationality, age, or sex of the speaker, but we know that sometimes they do. You can't always count on listeners being tolerant and free of prejudices. You certainly have a right to object if that happens to you, but complaining does not help the audience get the message. What can you do if you perceive that your listeners are rejecting you because of something over which you have no control? *Solution:* Don't react in anger. You have nothing to gain by expressing hostility to an audience; in fact, doing that may reinforce their prejudices. Try if you can to penetrate the stereotype by projecting yourself as a person who is different from their preconceived notions. If you speak intelligently and convey a sense of reason and responsibility, you may succeed in gaining their respect in the long run.

Are we making progress in this area? Let's hope so. There was a time when black people could not even vote, let alone run for office; in many states women were not permitted to sit on a jury; long-haired men were not moved into corporate executive positions; and homosexuals were forced to resign from public service jobs. These conditions began to change when articulate people who belonged to such minority groups were able to break through the barriers of prejudice and convince those in positions of power that race, gender, hair style, and sexual orientation had nothing to do with a person's character or ability.

Observe the Time Limit

Any person in show business will tell you that timing is one of the most essential ingredients of a successful performance; the same is true of public speaking. If your speech runs long, the audience may stop listening before you reach your conclusion. Even though they may politely remain in their seats, nothing is getting through to them after they have shut off their auditory receptors. Studies tell us that the attention of an audience peaks in the first twenty minutes of a presentation and begins to taper off after that. Does that mean that speeches should never be longer than twenty minutes? No. But you may have to work harder for attention if you are demanding a lot of the audience's time. Failure to observe the time limit became an embarrassment to Governor Bill Clinton of Arkansas when he was delivering the nominating speech for presidential candidate Michael Dukakis during the 1988 Democratic convention. Clinton was supposed to speak for fifteen minutes; instead he talked for three-quarters of an hour. Delegates who were eager to hear the acceptance speech of the Democratic candidate began to shuffle about and whisper chiding remarks. Finally Clinton came to the end and began his closing by saying, "In conclusion . . . ," whereupon the audience immediately began to cheer. In fairness, we must observe that Governor Clinton is a capable person and had some important things to say that would have been well received on another occasion. But in this situation his timing was bad. What we can learn is that regardless of how vital your information may be, there is no point in talking if no one is listening. *Solution:* Never go beyond the time that has been scheduled for you. Keep the speech as tight as you can; if you have a lot to say, you may have to talk at a fairly brisk rate. Don't go into so much detail that members of the audience miss the main point; they will listen better if your material is concentrated. The more time you consume, the greater risk you take of losing their attention.

RESPECT FOR THE AUDIENCE

Keep in mind that your function as a speaker is to meet the needs of the audience. You are on the platform for their benefit, not for your own. You may be getting certain rewards from the experience—it may be gratifying and fulfilling—but basically your purpose is to provide information that your listeners can use. If your audience is willing to accept your assertions, you can take satisfaction for having achieved your objective, but if they don't, you must remember that they have the right to disagree. There is no way you can force your message on them. You have an opportunity to be heard, but there is no guarantee that your message will succeed in persuading them. People will listen so long as they believe it is in their interest to do so. If you try to demand attention, you will probably meet with resistance. Recognize the fact that communication is a shared experience and can be accomplished only when the rights of both the speaker and the listener are acknowledged and respected.

THE AUDIENCE'S BILL OF RIGHTS

We, the people of the audience, in order to form a more perfect speaking environment, establish clarity, ensure attention and interest, provide common understanding, promote communication, and secure the blessings of reason and logic for ourselves and our fellow listeners, do ordain and establish this Bill of Rights for the Public Forums of America.

Article I

No speaker shall come to the podium unprepared. The speaker shall have given thought to the issue and shall be equipped with notes and visual aids as required.

Article II

The information contained in the speech shall be significant and useful. No excessive trivialities shall prevail on the podium.

Article III

The speaker shall tell the truth and nothing but the truth, and shall not intentionally deceive the audience by omitting necessary information.

Article IV

The speaker shall be punctual and not unnecessarily delay the audience. The speech shall begin and end on time.

Article V

The speaker shall articulate clearly and speak in a voice loud enough for all to hear. Attention shall be given even to those in the back of the room.

Article VI

The speaker shall be courteous to the audience at all times during the main address and during the question period.

THE SPEAKER'S RIGHTS

In accordance with this Bill, the speaker's rights shall not be abridged by the audience. Members of the audience shall not heckle or create distractions that interfere with the speaker's thoughts. The audience shall listen attentively even though they disagree with the speaker's viewpoint. They shall participate during the question period with directness and brevity. They shall not make speeches of their own from the floor.

EXERCISE

Survey the class members and gather demographic information that will provide a statistical profile of the audience you will be addressing. Find out the average age, ratio of men to women, nationalities represented, number of married people, and average amount of time students spend working for pay. In your survey ask how many students voted in the last election and to what political party they are registered. You might also want to inquire about religious affiliations by having them check one of the predominant categories: Catholic, Protestant, Jewish, Muslim, Hindu, Buddhist, other, or none. After this information has been compiled, write it up on a chalkboard where everyone can see it; then conduct a class discussion and speculate on the generalizations a speaker could make about the possible reactions the class might have to various topics and points of view.

QUESTIONS FOR REVIEW

1 What do we mean by the *demographics* of an audience?

2 What do we mean by the *logistics* of the speaking occasion?

3 How might age differences affect the way a speaker's message is received?

4 How can cultural diversity in a classroom be an asset to students of public speaking?

5 How does the term *personal relevance* relate to changes in attitude and belief structure? What does a speaker need to do if the personal relevance factor is strong?

6 What is meant by the *peripheral route* to cognitive change? If the personal relevance factor is not strong, how might a speaker bring about change in a person's belief structure?

7 What is meant by a *single-issue voter*? What effect do single-issue voters have on political candidates?

8 How much of our waking time is spent in communication? How much involves listening?

9 What are some of the bad habits that interfere with good listening?

10 What does a speaker need to do before launching into the main idea of the message?

11 What do we mean when we say the purpose statement should be qualified?

12 What are several ways to emphasize key words and important points?

13 What are some ways of holding the listener's attention?

14 What do we mean by *stereotypes*? How can they be overcome?

15 What might be the consequences of speaking beyond your time limit?

PART TWO

THE MESSAGE

The Speech to Inform If you were delivering your speech in a classroom or lecture hall, you would probably be giving a speech to inform. Almost all speeches contain some information, but the speech to inform has that characteristic as its primary function. A speech falls into this category if you are making an effort to present your material objectively without trying to persuade your audience to take a particular point of view. The subject matter might deal with controversial material, but when you are giving a speech to inform, you are not trying to influence the decision of the audience one way or another. You are simply giving them the information they need to make up their own minds. Sometimes you hear this approach referred to as an *expository* speech.

The Speech to Convince If you were making a speech in a courtroom or legislative hearing room, you would probably be giving a speech to convince. Your purpose would be to try to persuade your audience to think favorably about your cause and to accept the point of view that you want them to take. You would still be giving information to your listeners, but adding an interpretation that would lead them to a particular conclusion. In this type of speech you would expect opposition, and you would be prepared to refute it. You would probably be using both emotional and logical appeals.

The Speech to Motivate This is the kind of speech that is designed to inspire people. When it is given by a preacher and delivered from a pulpit, it is called a "sermon" or a "homily." It might also be a presentation made by a marketing manager who is introducing a new promotional campaign or is trying to generate enthusiasm on the part of the sales staff. It may contain some factual evidence, but the most successful speeches of this kind rely heavily on appeals to universal values, metaphorical language, and illustrations that reach people at the emotional level. The audience would probably be people who already agree with the basic premise of the speaker but are looking for inspiration. The purpose here is to move people to action: to live a better life, to work for a cause, to contribute their money, to join an organization, or to vote for a candidate.

The Speech to Entertain If you were an actor or a comedian and liked to perform on the stage, you might be asked to give a speech to entertain. Such a presentation is often referred to as an "after dinner speech" and is designed primarily for the sake of amusement. You would not expect the audience to learn anything of significance or to be persuaded to a point of view; you would simply want them to enjoy the experience. This kind of speech generally consists of humorous references, anecdotes, and narrations worked around a central theme. It is appropriate when an audience is in a relaxed or perhaps frivolous mood.

The general purpose of the speech should be clear in your own mind, but you don't necessarily have to state what it is. It's not a good idea to say to your audience, "My purpose is to convince you . . . ," because you may set up resistance to what you want to accomplish. Often your general purpose will be suggested by the nature of the occasion. The person who invites you to speak will give you some indication by asking you to explain a procedure, support a recommendation, get a program moving, or lighten the mood of the audience. Try to accommodate your listeners by giving them what they want and what they expect. It is not good form to launch into a persuasive speech when you have been asked simply to provide information.

SELECTING THE TOPIC

If public speaking is a new experience for you, selecting the topic may seem at first to be difficult. Begin by thinking of things with which you have had direct experience—hobbies, travels, jobs, recreational interests, etc. Consider also topics that you have studied or read about in books and periodicals. You might want to speak about the profession or vocation you plan to enter, or perhaps about a charitable cause that you support. As you begin listing possibilities, you may be surprised at how many subjects there are that you can talk about. Here are a few suggested topics to get you started.

- Cross-country travel on a mountain bike
- The potential of electric automobiles
- Making movies with a camcorder
- Investing money in the stock market
- The culture of the Navajo Indians
- Irrigating farmlands in arid regions

If you are called on to make a speech on a controversial topic, your best source of ideas would probably be the front page of the daily newspaper. Possible topics might include issues such as the following:

- Covert operations of the CIA
- Negotiating a settlement in the Israeli-Palestinian dispute
- A national health care program in the United States
- Banning assault weapons
- Making birth control devices available in high schools
- Requiring drug tests for professional athletes

There are many others that you will be able to add to the list once you begin thinking about them. What you will discover as you begin developing your ideas for the controversial topic is that it is easier to describe the problem than it is to recommend a solution. We'll discuss that further in the chapter on persuasion.

Appropriateness

In selecting a topic, be sure to consider the way the audience is likely to perceive your information. You may intend to give an expository speech on human fossils found to be a million years old; however, your claims could be regarded as controversial by those who believe in the biblical story of creation. This is when you need to remember that the message that matters is the message that is received.

Complexity

Another thing to consider when selecting your topic is the complexity of the subject matter. You may know a great deal about a theoretical concept in physics or mathematics, but if the audience does not have the background that you do, your explanations might be too difficult for them to understand. Subjects that are extremely complex often lend themselves more to individual instruction than to public address. Giving a speech that is way over the heads of the listeners leads people to believe that you are trying to make an impression by showing off your knowledge.

Significance

If you are working on a speech to inform, convince, or motivate, select a topic that has some significance. Don't waste your time or the time of the audience on trivialities. You don't want to go beyond the listeners' capabilities for comprehension, but you don't want to insult their intelligence either. If you are giving a speech to entertain and your sole purpose is to provide amusement, you can take whatever topic you want, provided that you can make it funny and that the people in the audience know what they have come to hear.

Scope

Don't overestimate the amount of material you can cover in the time you are allowed. If the subject area you are considering is too broad, you may find yourself under too much pressure to include everything you want to say. Bring your topic into focus. That means narrow the scope so that you have enough time to elaborate on the points you want to make. For example, you cannot give an effective speech on the history of aviation. You might, however, be able to talk about the work of flight attendants on commercial aircraft.

GATHERING INFORMATION

How do people acquire the information they include in speeches? They do it by recalling what they already know; by traveling or getting involved in an activity; by talking to others who are informed on the topic; by watching a play, a movie, or a TV documentary; and certainly by reading books and periodicals. When you are studying public speaking at the college level, much of the information you gather will come from the library, so plan on spending a good deal of time there. Be sure you start your research early; you may find that the topic is more complex than you had thought. You might also discover that the point of view you wanted to express is not so supportable as it seemed to be; in fact, what you read might change your thinking altogether. Begin your research with an open mind, and allow the information you gather to lead you to your conclusion. You will want not only the most reliable data, but also the most current. The

Much of the information you need is available through computer access.

best place to look is in the periodicals. Here are a few indexes, which are the basic tools of research.

Computer Access to Periodicals

In most libraries today many of the articles appearing in the periodicals you will need can be found through a computer terminal. The system might be called "Magazine Index" or perhaps "InfoTrac." It will be able to access 400 or so periodicals plus newspapers such as the *New York Times*. To find the sources, simply enter a subject title and press the SEARCH key. A list of articles will appear on the screen, and you can pick the ones you want.

Readers' Guide to Periodical Literature

This is the old-fashioned index that is still reliable, even during power failures. It comes in bound volumes with updated pamphlets. You'll find it useful if your library does not have computer access or if you are looking for an article that is more than ten years old. Titles, authors, and subject headings are listed alphabetically with cross-references; it indexes about 150 popular periodicals.

Social Science Index; Humanities Index

These references are cross-indexed by title, author, and subject headings similar to the *Readers' Guide*; they will direct you to the more scholarly articles and recent studies that appear in professional journals such as *Political Science Quarterly* and the *Journal of Philosophy*.

Education Index; Business Index

These reference volumes are also arranged in the same way as the *Readers' Guide*, and they are just as easy to use. They will lead you to professional journals dealing with recent studies, experiences, and theories in the field of education and in business.

New York Times Index

This is an extremely useful library reference that can be used when you know the approximate time of an event but want specific information about the details. The volumes are arranged according to subject and in chronological sequence. You will find a brief summary of the event itself and also a reference to the *New York Times* edition that carried the story in detail. For in-depth research, you could go into the archives of the newspaper and retrieve the original article.

Psychological Abstracts

This index refers you to articles that have appeared in professional journals covering the field of psychology. It tells you the name of the author, the publication, and the date and also gives a brief summary of the conclusions that were drawn in the study. To read the details of the material, you would have to look up the periodical and find the article itself.

Social Issues Resources Series

This source is not an index but contains the actual information. It includes current articles arranged in chronological order and covers thirty-two subject areas. It will provide you with the description and scope of a given problem, definitions, an analysis of causes, and possible solutions. It is supplemented with new material every year. Some of the social issues included are crime, family, population, human rights, and others that are frequently used as speech topics.

Reference Books

There are a great many other sources you can use for background information: the *World Almanac*, *Facts on File*, and *Statistical Abstract of the United States*, to name just a few. As you progress in your college work, learn to use research tools other than just encyclopedias and dictionaries. And by all means, don't hesitate to ask the librarian for assistance.

Taking Notes

Library research can be time-consuming and still not be productive if you fail to keep track of what you read. The beginning speech student may spend many hours in the library poring over books and periodicals, yet fail to include any concrete information in the speech. Don't rely on your memory alone; take notes as you read. Record names of people, places, and things; professional titles and positions; dates and times; costs and quantities; court cases and scientific studies; and any details you might need to put into your outline to help you develop and substantiate the explanations or historical accounts you plan to include in the speech. Be sure you make note of the sources you use in gathering your information. On some occasions the audience may be skeptical about what you tell them, and the quality of the source may determine their willingness to accept it.

If you find that your research takes a good deal of time and effort, you are probably going about it in the right way. The presentations you make in class are certainly going to require a lot of work, but the most rigorous kind of speech preparation is that which is made for a religious sermon. Theologian Charles L. Allen advises as a rule of thumb that ministers spend "an hour in the study for every minute in the pulpit."[1]

FORMS OF SUPPORT

A speech that is well-balanced is one that has variety in its development. You would not want to have a speech that is composed entirely of quotations or statistics, although those are both substantial forms of elaboration. Let's examine the kinds of supporting material that you can look for when you are gathering information and taking notes on what you want to include in the speech.

Definitions

In order for the audience to understand what you say, the level of your vocabulary must not be over their heads. Words, phrases, and terminology that are new to them or outside their frame of reference must be explained. While you are in the process of gathering your information, make note of what you think may need to be defined.

Technical Words   A speech dealing with scientific matters is difficult for members of an audience to understand if they do not have a technical background. Listeners may give up trying to follow you if the terminology is not clear. In a speech on sources of energy, for example, reference to "cold fusion" as it pertains to atomic physics would need to be defined in a way that a nontechnical person would be able to comprehend.

Legal Terms   If you were giving a speech dealing with a constitutional issue, there might be legal terms that you would have to define such as *reasonable doubt* or *probable cause.* Ordinary reference books would not be much help; you would have to consult a source such as *Black's Law Dictionary.*

Words in Other Languages   We are used to people's borrowing words from other languages when the English word is not adequate to convey the idea. We all know what is meant when we hear the Hawaiian word *aloha* or the Hebrew expression *shalom.* But if the foreign word is not well

[1] "American Preaching: A Dying Art?" *Time,* Dec. 31, 1979, p. 64.

known, it requires definition. Jaime Escalante, the math teacher whose story was portrayed in the movie *Stand and Deliver* uses the Spanish word *ganas* to describe the importance of his students' having a strong desire and motivation to learn. When he speaks to an audience, he takes the time to define the word because it plays an important part in his teaching method.

Common Words with Specialized Meanings   We may think we know the meaning of a word, but if it is used in a specialized way, we may not understand it at all. In education, for example, the word *articulation* refers to the arrangements two schools make to coordinate their programs.

Words Defined by Quantitative Measure   If you were to favor giving federal aid to people living in poverty, you would have to define quantitatively what you meant by the term *poverty*. In this case the definition is continually changing as the cost of living changes. In 1990 the Census Bureau set the poverty level at $13,359 per year for an urban family of four. You can see how the number of people considered to be living in poverty could be modified by raising or lowering that economic index.

Specific Instances

As you read, look for specific instances that are interesting and are related to the point you want to make. Include details of the illustration to add credibility to your statement. You may wish to cite a number of such examples or take just one and elaborate on it. If your topic is controversial, you will have to point out how the incident you have selected leads to the conclusion you want to draw. This kind of rhetorical support is sometimes called *anecdotal*, and it is an excellent device for gaining and holding the attention of the audience. People like to listen to stories, particularly those that have unusual or mysterious characteristics.

Sometimes theories are based on anecdotal support: For example, the mystery of the Bermuda Triangle was created by an Associated Press reporter named E. V. W. Jones. He noted an instance that occurred on December 5, 1945, when five Navy torpedo bombers took off from a base in Fort Lauderdale, Florida, and were never seen or heard of again. The incident by itself may not have attracted extraordinary attention, but Jones discovered that there were a number of other mysterious disappearances that also occurred in the same triangle marked by Bermuda, Puerto Rico, and Fort Lauderdale. The story captured the imagination of people all over the world.

Anecdotes are fun and interesting for the storyteller as well as for the audience, but let's make sure we put their value and significance in perspective. By themselves they can not *prove* a generalization; they are simply indicators that a condition may exist. Sometimes people jump too quickly to conclusions based on anecdotal support without asking for more substantial evidence. Medical theories, for example, may be based on instances when people were cured of a disease by a particular herb or vitamin. The theory may begin to develop credibility if there are a great many instances that produce the same result, but unless there are controlled studies to verify the theory, the scientific world is generally skeptical.

Controlled Studies

When we conduct a controlled study, we are using what is called the *scientific method*. We would start with a hypothesis or a theory. Then we would proceed to test it by setting up a series of experiments in which we control all the variables. By modifying one variable at a time and observing the results, we begin to learn what the outcome will be when a particular adjustment is made. To find out what causes cancer in rats, for example, we control the conditions of their environment and then proceed to make one change at a time in their diet or exposure to chemical substances. If we get to a point where we can repeat the experiment and are able to predict what result will be produced by a particular change, we say that the study has "reliability."

As an undergraduate college student you may not be called upon to conduct original research; you can simply examine the studies that have already been made. But you want to know how such studies are conducted so that you are able to tell if your information is really substantial. Studies conducted in physics and chemistry, of course, are going to be more reliable than those conducted in the behavioral sciences; however, the same methodology is used. Studies frequently have to be qualified by language that acknowledges the fact that there are exceptions to the generalizations being made. You can cite studies, for example, which show that smoking cigarettes causes lung cancer, but you would have to acknowledge that there are people who smoke who do not get cancer, and there are people who get cancer who do not smoke. But even though there are exceptions, scientific studies provide us with more reliable information than do casual observations we might make.

Statistical Examples

The term *statistical examples* means any kind of information that can be expressed in numbers. It is sometimes called *quantitative information*—evidence that can be counted or measured. It may be in the form of totals, percentages, averages, rates, or other numerical values. It can be obtained by actual count or from random samples. Statistics may be important to establish the validity of a claim. If you provide no quantitative evidence, your audience may begin to believe that you are simply trying to sell them "blue-sky" notions that have no substantive meaning. Consider the following claims that a speaker might make:

1 "There is a great deal of oil that can still be drilled off the coast of California."

2 "Most people are in favor of capital punishment."

3 "Students who go to Catholic schools score higher on achievement tests than those who go to public schools."

All these claims require quantitative support; specific instances or anecdotal evidence alone would not be sufficient. In the first example, you might report on the barrels of oil that have already been pumped from one well, but to make the claim that a lot is still available requires an estimate from an expert in the field who has conducted reliable studies. Even if we had that figure, we might also want to know how much that is in comparison with other oil fields, and how long it would last at the present rate of consumption.

The second statement would also have to be supported by statistical information. It would not be enough to ask eight or ten people if they favored capital punishment. You would have to present figures gathered from a recent survey that was conducted using a random or representative sample of a given population. And then you would have to restrict your generalization so that it applied to people in the particular area that was surveyed.

In order for the third statement to be an acceptable claim, you would have to compare the scores of the Catholic students with those of students in public schools. The comparison would have to be based on the same test given to a significant sample of students in the same time period.

Use statistics to support a generalization when it is necessary, but use them in such a way as to provide clarification and credibility for what you are saying. Here are some suggestions:

• Don't inundate your listeners with more statistics than they can retain. If you have a long list, put the figures on a chart for them to see, write them on a chalkboard, or distribute copies of a handout sheet. Doing this will help them remember and will also impress upon them that the numbers are important.

• Round off large numbers when it's possible to do so without distorting the information. An expenditure of $1,468,216.00 can be expressed in a speech more easily as "almost one and a half million dollars."

• Don't use figures deceptively. Avoid the habit of substituting percentages for adjectives. While you may have reason to believe that a large portion of the staff favors a four-day workweek, don't say "90 percent of the people on the staff like the idea" unless you have actually taken a survey.

• Don't compare absolute numbers with percentages. It is not very useful to say that a neighboring district cut its expenses by $200,000 while our reduction was only 6 percent.

Statistics can be misleading if you are not careful. Figures that show a rising crime rate may not necessarily indicate an increase in crime; they may merely reflect an increase in arrests. Records show that more automobile accidents are caused by men than by women. However, this doesn't mean that women are better drivers; it just means that men do more driving. Recognizing such fallacies in the use of statistics is not just the responsibility of the audience. It is also the responsibility of the ethical speaker.

The advantage of statistics is that they give the listener the "big picture" and add significance to your assertions. The danger is that statistics can be carelessly used. Numbers can be manipulated by words, as illustrated in the following example:

> Three men decided to share a hotel room that cost $30. They each paid the clerk $10 and went up to the room. Later, the clerk remembered that the room had been reduced in price to $25, so he told the bellhop to take $5 back to the three men. On the way up to the room the bellhop decided to keep $2 for a tip. He gave the men $3, so they each got a dollar back. The room then cost each man $9 instead of $10. Three times nine is twenty-seven; the bellhop kept $2. What happened to the other dollar?

In this example the arithmetic is accurate, but the conclusion is false because the words used to relate the story are deceptive. The same can be true when statistical information is used in a speech. Figures do not speak for themselves. The speaker has an obligation to interpret the figures in a responsible way so that they clarify an issue rather than obscure it.

The emphasis you place on the statistical data and the way you state the evidence will have a lot to do with the impact the numbers have on the listeners. For example, it may be true that in a single year a corporation doubled its profit. But it could also be true that its profits went from 1 percent to 2 percent. Both those statements might be perfectly accurate; yet their implications are significantly different.

Statistical data can often be confusing and difficult for the audience to remember. As a speaker, you can help listeners to understand and retain what you say by relating quantitative evidence to an example they can visualize. Consider the way Thomas R. Kuhn, president of Edison Electric Institute clarified his statistics when he spoke on the topic "Energy, Efficiency, Ingenuity":

> Thanks to the cumulative impact of these new energy sources, per capita energy consumption in the U.S. today is about 327 million Btu per year. That's 96,000

kWh. What does that mean to us? Look at it this way: The unassisted human body can do work equal to about 67 kWh per year. But each of us consumes 96,000 kWh a year. That's the equivalent of 1,433 workers. In other words, each of us has 1,433 servants.[2]

People can understand the meaning of the message, when statistics are phrased in this fashion, even if they are not familiar with the terms *Btu* and *kWh*. Also, the clear imagery will help them remember the data better than if the figures were given by themselves.

Testimonial Evidence

Much of the evidence you choose for your speech will not be quantitative and will need to be expressed in words rather than numbers. Again, you will want to go beyond your own experience and relate observations that have been made by other people. This type of support is called *testimonial evidence* and can be divided into several categories:

Eyewitness Accounts   Court trials rely heavily on this type of testimony. Witnesses will be called to describe in detail precisely what they saw or heard. They must testify only to that which they themselves actually experienced—what they were told by other people is called "hearsay evidence" and is not admissible. While eyewitness accounts are given great weight by judges and juries, such testimony is not infallible. Many experiments have been conducted showing that wide discrepancies can appear in the accounts of different witnesses to the same event. When there are several eyewitnesses who all testify to having seen the same thing, the evidence is very strong. But if one person saw something that no one else did, the evidence may be open to some question.

Expert Testimony   Often courts will call to the stand people who are referred to as "expert witnesses." These are people who have expertise in a particular field and are able to verify the results of a study, experiment, or observation. They are able to understand technical data and relate scientific findings that are pertinent to the case. A ballistics expert, for example, can testify that two bullets were fired from the same gun. The jury does not need to understand the technology of such a finding, only that an expert has testified to that effect.

Expert Opinion   In your speech you might want to cite an observation made by an expert to support your assertion, even though the thought ex-

---

[2] Thomas R. Kuhn, "Energy, Efficiency, Ingenuity," *Vital Speeches*, Aug. 15, 1991, p. 659.

pressed is only an opinion. If you were giving a speech comparing U.S. automobiles with those manufactured by the Japanese, for example, you might quote something said in *Consumer Reports* about the ease of handling or the comfort of the ride. While an opinion of that nature does not mean much coming from an ordinary driver, the same observation made by a recognized expert or reputable publication can be regarded rhetorically as supporting evidence.

Rules of Law

State and federal judges often use the word *opinion* in reference to a decision that has been made by the court, because the function of the judicial body of government is to interpret the laws of the land. But when opinions are expressed by the courts, they have more than just the power of influence; they carry the force of law. If you were to make this explanation in a speech, you might refer to the case of *Marbury v. Madison* in 1803, which gave power to the United States Supreme Court to rule on the constitutionality of legislative acts.

A rule of law could also be federal, state, or local legislation. Legal statutes often become important when you are speaking in a subject area pertaining to contemporary social issues. In a speech on the federal budget for example, you might want to cite the Gramm-Rudman Act in reference to the efforts made by Congress to control the national deficit.

Literary Quotes

Quotations can fall into the same category as testimonial evidence when their function is to provide factual evidence, but sometimes the value of a quote is simply to add artistic flavor to the speech. For example, you may not be able to find anything concrete to support your belief that opinions have rhetorical value, but you could include a quote by Thomas H. Huxley, who said, "There is no greater mistake than the hasty conclusion that opinions are worthless because they are badly argued." Use a *direct* quotation when the phrasing has a unique quality. You can change the wording and express the meaning as an *indirect* quote, but be sure you cite the author of the idea. Don't make the mistake that Senator Joseph Biden did when he carelessly neglected to give source credit in a speech to a phrase that listeners recognized as being the words of someone else.

Explanation

Much of what you will be doing in both the speech to inform and the speech to convince will be providing explanations. As the speaker, you must be sure you understand the material thoroughly yourself. You may look at explanations in a number of different ways.

Analysis   When we analyze something, we examine all its component parts. We try to discover how it functions, what contributed to its present condition, and what changing circumstance might affect it in the future. In order to justify a claim you want to make in a speech, you may have to explain how you arrived at a particular conclusion. If you have the opportunity to make firsthand observations, you can conduct your own analysis of an issue. Football coaches do this all the time when they watch the playback of a game. They observe what each player did on every down to learn why the outcome was what it was. From an analysis like this they can develop strategies for future games. Conducting an in-depth analysis on a more complex issue is probably not something you would be able to do as an individual, but instead, you might report on the analysis made by an institution or an expert in the field. The National Academy of Sciences recently completed a fifteen-month study on the greenhouse effect, which is a condition that traps harmful gases within our atmosphere. The academy's analysis was that the danger of the greenhouse effect was real, that it could adversely affect the weather patterns of the entire world, and that carbon dioxide produced by the burning of fossil fuels was the most serious offender. The value of an analysis of this kind is that it tells you what questions need to be asked in order to find a solution. How can we generate electricity in the quantity we need without producing carbon dioxide? Do we have to stop relying on the burning of fossil fuels? What other energy sources are available to us? Questions of this kind are extremely important in the process that leads to workable solutions.

Historical Background   While you are doing your research, try to think of what historical background your audience will need in order to understand the point you are trying to make. If you are speaking on an issue such as affirmative action or equal opportunity employment, for instance, you might need to explain that the turning point in our national policy came about as a result of the Supreme Court decision in *Brown v. the Topeka Board of Education* in 1954. In that ruling the Court said that the constitutional rights of black children were violated when state law required that they attend separate schools from white children, even though the facilities provided were equal. Ever since the end of the Civil War, the segregationists had claimed that it was the right of the states to determine whether or not separate facilities would be maintained for blacks and whites. Until 1954 the law allowed them to do that. Providing this kind of background information might be necessary if your audience is composed

While doing your research, think of the historical background your audience will need.

of people who are new to this country or perhaps are young and have not studied the social conditions of earlier generations.

Description   Another form of explanation is description. If you have the ability to paint word-pictures, you can create images in the minds of your listeners. You may want to tell what it is like living in an urban slum, or you might wish to describe the beauty of Yellowstone National Park. This form of rhetorical development can be extremely effective if you are skillful in selecting relevant details and using vivid language. Description can be a powerful persuasive device if employed for that purpose.

Narration   Examples can be conveyed to an audience simply by presenting the bare facts, but you can generate more interest and create a stronger impact by relating the information in narrative form. Consider the style used by Irving B. Harris in a speech on education that he delivered to the Forum of the City Club of Cleveland:

Five years ago I picked up a copy of the *New York Times* and read an account of an initiative taken by the Superintendent of Schools in Minneapolis. . . . In order to improve his school system, he did something radical. He decided he would not allow anyone to go into tenth grade unless the student had satisfactorily completed all his ninth grade work. He wanted to be sure that tenth grade classes would not be slowed down by students who were not capable of learning at the tenth grade level. He set up a matriculation test at the end of ninth grade and did the same thing for seventh grade, fifth grade, second grade, and kindergarten. And much to everyone's surprise, 10 percent of the kindergarten class flunked. . . . The *New York Times* as well as the parents were shocked.[3]

In order for a narration to be effective, it needs to have a "punch line" at the end so your audience will get the point. Narrations can come from your own experience, or you can recreate them from your sources. If you are quoting a story of this kind, remember that you must give the author credit.

Analogy   An effective aid to explanation is analogy. Most people can learn better when new information is compared to something they already understand. If you wanted to explain the flow of electricity through a wire, you might compare the concept to the flow of water through a pipe. In a speech on this subject you could say that the water's motion is called the "current," the pressure that pushes the water is the "voltage," the valve that controls the flow is the "resistance," and the work done by the water is the "power." With this picture in mind, the listener might be able to understand your explanation better.

In addition to simplifying complex material, analogies can also be used to add color and vividness to your language. In doing this, analogies make your points and the ideas you advance more likely to be remembered. In a speech on career planning, you may want to say that sometimes it is necessary to move on to a new occupation, even though there may be some risk in doing so. Your analogy could be to that of a circus aerialist who must let go of one trapeze and spend an agonizing few seconds in midair without any support before grabbing on to the next bar. Having established the analogy, you can reinforce the point by making reference to the trapeze artist again later in the speech.

Analogies can be used in comparing any two concepts that have similar characteristics. Suppose you wanted to recommend that the United States extend free or low-cost health insurance to all citizens. You could say that good health is just as important to the citizens in a democracy as a good education, and since we provide free public schools, we should also see that every citizen has access to affordable medical care.

To emphasize the need for a change in our social mores, you might make an extended analogy of the way the current period in U.S. history

---

[3] Irving B. Harris, "Education: Does It Make a Difference When You Start?" *Vital Speeches*, Apr. 1, 1990, pp. 372–373.

compares to that of the Roman Empire during the reign of Nero. In drawing such an analogy you could cite the deployment of military forces in foreign lands, mastery in building, preoccupation with physical contact sports, corruption in government, sexual freedom, etc. By using this form of support, you would be able to provide information not only about our own country but also about the Roman Empire.

INTEREST GRABBERS

In either the speech to inform or the speech to convince, it is necessary for the speaker to hold the listeners' attention. In doing your research and gathering your thoughts, look for interest grabbers—examples or references that not only are informative but will make the audience want to listen. Here are a few ideas along those lines:

Humor

This is one of the most effective means of establishing rapport with the audience. When you get people to laugh, they are actively participating in the communication process. To do this, you don't have to be a comedian, and you don't have to feel that you need to be funny all the way through the speech. But humorous references will do a lot toward gaining attention. One of my colleagues recently asked me if I believed in free speech. I told him that I certainly did. "That's good," he said, "because I'd like to have you give one to my class next week." Now that's not a real "knee slapper," and it may not even get a laugh, but it would serve to lead me into a few remarks about the First Amendment.

Suspense

The reason adventure stories are popular is that they keep us in suspense. We read or listen all the way to the end to find out what is going to happen. In the *Tales of the Arabian Nights*, Scheherazade was such a good storyteller that the king let her live, as long as she continued to keep him in suspense. Take a lesson from this ancient tale and learn to hold the attention of your audience by not revealing the ending of your story until you have built it to a climax. The same principle applies to telling jokes. Don't give away the punch line until you have the curiosity of the listener.

Unusual Examples

Not all examples have to be unusual ones, but if you are able to add a few that have really interesting features, you can change an ordinary speech into one that people will remember. Some topics lend themselves to unusual examples more than others. In a speech on new high-tech products, one student described a device manufactured by an electronics company that would help keep people from losing their credit cards. It was designed in such a way that it started playing a tune after it had been exposed to light for several minutes. It continued to play until it was programmed to stop. An added feature was that you could pick from a hundred tunes what you wanted it to play. Another example that a student included in a speech was a study showing that a flatworm could learn conditioned behavior more easily after it had been fed another flatworm that had already been conditioned. The speaker suggested that perhaps students could learn the material of the course more easily if the instructor were carved up and served to the members of the class.

Familiar References

Have you ever been daydreaming during a lecture and then snapped back to attention when the speaker mentioned the name of a friend, or a place you had visited, or an incident you were involved in? This is a phenomenon that good speakers recognize and use as an effective attention grabber. It's not always possible for you to know what will be familiar to your audience, but you can make some good guesses. To start with, you can use references to other speeches that have been made in class, personality traits of your instructor or other students, or names of local places and events. Mentioning the names of popular entertainers, musical groups, or sports figures is another way to get the attention of the audience, or you might tie your information to an item that has recently appeared in the news.

Personalized Connections

People generally pay attention to things that are going to affect them directly. This is why newspapers try to find a "local angle" when reporting the news. If the national economy is entering a period of recession, the first thing people want to know is whether or not there will be employment layoffs in their community. When the crisis in the Persian Gulf began to develop, there was great concern in every town in the United States over the possibility that the local reserve unit would be called up. When you are planning your speech, try to think of how you can respond to the question that you know will be in everyone's mind, "How is this event going to affect me and my family?"

SELECTING YOUR MATERIAL

At this point in the preparation stage you should have the material for your speech spread out in front of you. You have now completed what may be the hardest part of the process. The next thing you need to do is become as familiar as you can with your information. You may find that you have more than you can use. In that case, you will have to select the best and leave the rest for another occasion. Resist the temptation to squeeze it all in if you have too much; you don't want to run the risk of going over your time limit or talking so long that the audience loses interest.

On the other hand you may discover that you don't have as much information as you thought you did, and you don't have time to gather more. In that case, go with what you have and keep the speech short. Don't try to pad your material just to fill up the time. The quality of the speech is not determined by its length.

Your next step is going to be to arrange the information in a logical and coherent sequence, so make sure that the ideas you want to include are clear in your mind.

EXERCISE

Using the computer access terminal for periodical literature in your college library, prepare a bibliography of five sources of information pertaining to one of the speech topics suggested in this chapter. In addition, find an example from one or more magazines to illustrate the forms of support: definition, specific instance, controlled study, statistical example, testimonial evidence, rule of law, literary quote, and explanation.

QUESTIONS FOR REVIEW

1 What are the three general speech purposes?

2 What is meant by a *homily*? Where would you expect to hear such an address?

3 What is an *expository* speech?

4 What kind of speech might draw upon universal values and metaphorical language?

5 What do we mean by limiting the *scope* of the topic?

6 What are the names of systems that provide computer access to periodicals?

7 What other indexes do libraries have that will lead you to material found in periodicals?

8 In what sources would you look to find specific facts and statistical information?

9 Why is the quality of the source often as important as the information itself?

10 What is meant by *anecdotal* information?

11 What is meant by *quantitative* information?

12 Why do we say that figures do not speak for themselves?

13 How can you make statistical data more meaningful to the audience?

14 In a court trial what is meant by *expert testimony*?

15 What is the value of using analogy as a means of support?

16 What are "interest grabbers," and what value do they have in a speech?

THE ORGANIZATIONAL STRUCTURE

Your main responsibility as a speaker is to present information to your audience that is organized well enough so that they will be able to understand it and find a place for it in their own thinking. That's not an easy task considering the huge quantity of data that is available to us on almost any given topic. Information has, in fact, become the principal economic commodity of our social structure:

> The year 1956 was one of prosperity, productivity, and industrial growth for Americans . . . for the first time in American history, white-collar workers in technical, managerial and clerical positions outnumbered blue-collar workers. Industrial America was giving way to a new society, where, for the first time, most of us worked with information rather than producing goods.[1]

The chances are very good that you will become employed by a company, either in the public or in the private sector, which generates, assimilates, and dispenses information. Since over half the working population of the country is doing the same thing, you can imagine the mountain of data that is being produced.

Good organization is essential to effective speaking for three reasons: It will allow you to convey a lot of information in a short period of time, it will permit your audience to follow you more easily and retain what you have to say, and it will minimize the risk of your forgetting what you plan to cover. Knowing that you have the sequence of your ideas clearly in

---

[1] John Naisbitt, *Megatrends*, Warner Books, New York, 1982, p. 2.

mind will also ease the speech anxiety that comes from the fear of forgetting something.

THE VALUE OF AN OUTLINE

Writing an outline is the most effective means of organizing your material because you can see the structure of what you want to say. Plan on making a rough draft first; you can't expect to get all your ideas down on paper in a neat, well-organized fashion the first time. When you do make your final copy, you may decide it is something you want to keep and use on more than just one occasion.

The Basic Structure

The outline you develop will be composed of several divisions. Think of them as boxes that you are going to use for the sake of sorting out your material.

INTRODUCTION

> **A** Attention statement
> **B** Purpose statement

BODY

> **I** Main heading
>   **A** Specific development
>   **B** Specific development
>   (Transition)

> **II** Main heading
>   **A** Specific development
>   **B** Specific development
>   (Transition)

CONCLUSION

> **A** Summary statement
> **B** Reinforcement of thesis

Each box has a specific purpose: In the one called "introduction" you will need material that will both gain the attention of the audience and tell them what you will be talking about. Each of the boxes labeled "body" will contain a main idea, supporting information, and a transition statement that leads to the next idea. In the box called "conclusion" you will put material that will summarize or reinforce the main idea of the speech. Let's look at each of those elements separately.

THE ATTENTION STATEMENT

Remember, we said that an audience is often inclined to tune in late; therefore, it's not a good idea to start right off with a purpose statement. You don't want to run the risk that your listeners will be thinking about something else when you provide for them the orientation to your topic. The first thing you need to do is to make sure that the audience is listening, so plan a statement that gains their attention. There are several ways you can do this:

- **The humorous anecdote** is a fairly standard method because laughter helps to relax both the audience and the speaker. When you get a response from your listeners early in the presentation, you will feel more confident knowing that you are off to a good start. Make sure, however, that your funny story has a point to it that is related to the purpose of the speech. It's quite possible that your anecdote will not get a laugh. If that happens, you are still all right as long as you can relate the punch line to something you want to say in the speech. Be cautious about off-color jokes; they may backfire if the audience does not appreciate blue humor. The same applies to ethnic or sexist jokes; they could do a great deal of damage to your integrity.

- **An illustrative anecdote** is an introduction that can be used if you don't want to begin by setting a mood of levity. In all cases, when you relate a story of any kind, plan the way you are going to tell it; think especially of how it should start and how it will end. The impact of all anecdotes, humorous or serious, depends on the phrasing of the punch line or climactic statement.

- **A surprising fact or claim** is a device that works well because it creates what might be called the "gee whiz" effect. For example, you might begin a speech on the importance of print journalism by calling attention to the fact that there are fewer words in a thirty-minute television newscast than there are on the front page of the *Wall Street Journal*. That fact could also be used as substantiating evidence in the body of the speech, but because of its surprising nature it is more valuable as an attention statement.

You have to gain and maintain the attention of your audience.

- **A rhetorical question** is an opening line that you can use when you want to gain the audience's attention before you advance an argument or an assertion. For example, you might begin by saying, "Why does the United States—a nation that spends more money on education than any other nation in the world—have such a high rate of illiteracy?" When you pose a rhetorical question, you are not asking for a response from the audience, you are leading into what you want to say. Such a question serves as a transition as well as a method of gaining attention.
- **A response question** is used when you want answers from the audience. You might begin by asking, "How many of you have lived in this community for more than ten years?" When you say this, raise your own hand to indicate what it is that you want the people to do. This method is quite effective because the audience becomes actively involved, and those who respond help you gain the attention of the others. What's more, you can tell by the show of hands if they are really listening.
- **Reference to the occasion** is an easy way to get started. You can begin by thanking the person who introduced you and letting the audience know that you are happy to have the opportunity to address them. If the day is a special occasion—an anniversary or the beginning of an event—let people know you are aware of that. If you can make a connection, tie the occasion into the topic of your speech.

Any of these methods can be used as an attention-getting device. The important thing is for you to give the audience an opportunity to get ready to listen.

THE PURPOSE STATEMENT

Once you have gained the audience's attention, you can move on to the second phase of the introduction—stating the purpose. This is the most important part of the speech because it is at this point that you provide the audience with orientation to your topic. You let your listeners know where you are going and how you are going to get there. To do that you should try to phrase your statement so that it is brief, clear, and well-qualified.

Brief. You don't want to go into detail right at the outset, because people will think you are beginning your speech in the middle. The body of the speech is the time for you to elaborate on your purpose statement.

Clear. Don't use sentence structure that is too long and complicated. The audience must be able to understand your intent, or else they will lose interest right at the start.

Well-qualified. This means that you tell your listeners how you have limited the subject matter and what you are going to emphasize. Sometimes this is referred to as the *parameters* of the topic.

Since the purpose statement is so important, let's start at the very beginning, when you are deciding on what the substance of your speech will be.

Giving Focus to the Subject

Your interest and involvement in a particular subject or activity may be the reason for your being invited to speak. Perhaps you have been serving as a volunteer for a community welfare group, and a local service club has learned about the work you are doing. The program chairperson calls you and says that the organization she represents is interested in learning more about poverty in America. Right away you can see that a topic of that magnitude is much too broad in scope for any kind of effective report, and it may be that your experience is not that comprehensive. Subjects that fall under the heading of "poverty in America" could include the chronically indigent, unemployment, shelters for the homeless, the food stamp program, public day care centers, institutions for the mentally ill, and medical facilities for the physically handicapped, to name just a few. It might be that your work has been primarily in helping families in poverty, and you want to confine your remarks to that segment of the problem. You can suggest to the program chairperson that the topic of your talk could be financial aid to families with dependent children. When you focus your subject that way, you provide for yourself a topic that is manageable.

Your own experience may be your primary source of information, but in addition to that you might need to gather more material from the library. Look under such headings as "welfare assistance," "aid to families," and "children in poverty." Be sure that you don't confine yourself to just one source, because you want this presentation to be distinctly your own. As you begin to read and take notes, you may discover that there is a particular aspect of the issue that is especially urgent, and you may be able to narrow your topic still further. For example, you might learn that the people who are hit the hardest by poverty conditions are single parents. Let the information you find lead you to your thesis. When you have gathered the material you want to use, you are ready to write your purpose statement.

Phrasing the Purpose Statement

The purpose statement is the keystone of the speech; it lets your audience know what it is that you are going to talk about. If the topic is controversial, it would be called a *thesis statement* and it will prepare them for the point of view you want to express. The statement brings the subject area into focus and lets the listeners know what limitations you have placed on the topic. Give a lot of consideration to the way you phrase the purpose statement; it is important to the audience, but it is also important to you. It will help you get a good, firm handle on what it is that you intend to say. I suggest that you write the purpose statement on your outline pretty much the way you plan to say it, and keep it in the back of your mind the whole time you are delivering the speech. *Everything you say should be related to that purpose statement.* If you follow that guideline, you will be less likely to go off on tangents that are not related to the central idea of the speech. Here are several ways you can phrase the purpose statement. Notice that each has a different emphasis and suggests a slightly different focus.

- A great many single parents in the United States are struggling to rear their families alone, and are often in need of financial assistance.
- Since the 1960s there has been an increase in single-parent families, and financial assistance is still not adequate.
- It's important that we learn the needs of single-parent families and how we can help in their struggle to survive.
- We need to provide assistance to single-parent families in the cities, in the suburbs, and in the rural areas.
- There are several ways that single-parent families in need can receive material assistance.

The Presummary

The purpose statement gives the audience a general idea of what aspect of the topic you plan to cover, but you also may need to tell your listeners how the speech is organized and what sequence you will follow as you progress from one point to another. To do that, you add what is called a *presummary*. This is a list of the main ideas that will be contained in the body of the speech. On your outline you would write just a few words to suggest briefly what you are going to say:

> Today I would like to describe to you
>
>   **1** The extent of the problem
>   **2** The financial need of single parents
>   **3** Some alternative solutions that might work better than what we are doing

In order for the audience to listen well, they must be able to recognize the speaker's organizational pattern. The presummary will help them do this. Be sure that the items listed in your presummary follow the same sequence as your main headings. The main headings form the basic skeleton of the speech, and they need to be arranged in a pattern that accomplishes the intent of the purpose statement.

THE MAIN HEADINGS

To organize your material you will need to divide your information into categories; each category will have a *main heading*. The main heading can also be called a "generalization," and it consists of a statement that summarizes all the information listed under it. The main headings must follow some sort of logical organizational structure. The following are a few possible patterns, using the welfare topic as an example.

The Problem-Solution Pattern   The first heading makes the claim that the problem is a significant one; the second heading addresses the needs and the causes; the third heading suggests alternatives and possible solutions.

• A great many single parents in the United States are struggling to rear their families alone, and often they are in need of financial assistance.

> **I** The problem of single-parent families has increased in recent years.
> **II** Single parents generally lose income and often face poverty unless they receive welfare.
> **III** State and local programs may work better than federal assistance.

Main headings will help the audience follow the organizational pattern of your speech.

The Chronological Pattern   Here the organizational pattern follows a historical progression. You start with the earliest incidents and proceed to those that are the most current.

- Since the 1960s there has been an increase in single-parent families, and financial assistance is still not adequate.
  I We recognized the problem in the mid 1960s.
  II The problem became acute in the 1970s as the divorce rate rose.
  III Workable solutions did not get started until the 1980s.

If your speech focuses just on the solution, you might use the chronological pattern so that it progresses from the first step to the second step to the third step.

- It's important that we learn the needs of single-parent families and how we can help in their struggle to survive.
  I First we must provide facilities for the family's basic survival.
  II Next we need to teach coping skills to the child and to the parent.
  III Finally, we need programs to help parents get off welfare.

The Spatial Pattern   The problem you are describing might differ from one locale to another, in which case you could use the spatial pattern for organizing your material. Notice that the example below could also be one that moves from most severe to least severe.

- We need to provide assistance to single-parent families in the cities, in the suburbs, and in the rural areas.
  I Single parenthood is a severe problem in the metropolitan areas.
  II The suburbs have their share of single parents, but facilities are better.
  III Rural areas have the least problem, but it still exists.

The Topical Pattern   Often your material will break down into clearly divided subject areas that form a natural organizational pattern. The example below could be used when you are giving an informational speech to a group of people who are interested in applying for welfare.

- There are three ways that single-parent families in need can receive material assistance.
  I Help can come from federally funded programs.
  II Help can come from state and local agencies.
  III Help can come from church groups and private organizations.

What we are doing here is one of the most important steps in speech preparation: We are providing the *structure* of the speech. There are several things you should note: The main headings are designated by roman numerals; you want to make sure they stand out and are easily recognized when you deliver the speech. Secondly, they are generalizations, not statements of fact. Make them broad enough to cover what you want to say, but not so vague as to be meaningless. For example, don't use this as a main heading:

II Let me give you some statistics about divorce.

That kind of statement does not help the audience understand what you mean. Instead use this:

II The high divorce rate accounts for a large part of the problem.

Having said that, you can proceed to give your statistics.

Each main heading requires supporting information; it cannot stand alone. Limit the number of main headings; if you have too many, your speech becomes fragmented. I suggest not working with more than five. And remember that the main headings must be directly related to what is said in the thesis or purpose statement of the speech.

Transitions

The organizational structure of your speech is going to be clear to you because you are the one who planned it, and you can see what it looks like on the outline in front of you. You know that there are divisions in the speech and that each division has a main idea; you also know the point at which you complete one main idea and begin to develop another one. However, this may not be so clear to the audience as it is to you. In order for them to be able to follow the flow of your organizational structure, you have to provide signposts for them, which we call *transitions*. A transition is a phrase that leads the audience into your next idea. You might say, for example, "But there are other problems to consider . . ." or "Now in order for us to understand, we need to look at . . ." As you begin to get more experience in public speaking, you will develop a sense for where transitions need to go. Transitions do not have to be written down in your outline; they are easy enough to extemporize, so long as you are aware of their importance.

SUPPORTING INFORMATION

Each main heading is really a minithesis; it answers the question "What is the point you want to make?" You might look at each one as an internal summary statement that helps the audience follow the progression of your ideas. But we said that main headings cannot stand alone; they need to be supported by specific information.

The kind of information you need to support your main headings is that which was described in the previous chapter: definition of terms, specific instances, statistical data, testimonial evidence, and explanation. You should have notes in front of you that contain the information which will become the development of each of your main headings. Your job now is to figure out where each piece of information fits. Here are some data you might want to include in the speech:

- Over half of all marriages end in divorce.
- Eighty-seven percent of black children live in mother-only families.
- The average income of single parents is $10,000 to $14,000.
- Three and a half million families are headed by women alone.
- One out of every five children will be born to unwed parents.
- If the mother keeps the child, she generally rears it alone.
- Forty-five percent of white children are reared by mothers only.
- Over 11,000 women have been through the program.

Would you present the material the way it is listed here? If not, how would you arrange it? You will see how this is done when you look at the sample outline, but first there is one more step you have to take before the outline of your speech is finished—planning the conclusion.

THE CONCLUSION

When you reach the end of the presentation, you will have to let the audience know you have finished. If you conclude with a piece of specific information such as "Over 11,000 women have been through the program," the audience is going to look at you expecting you to say something more. You can't end a speech that way; you need to pull your ideas together either by summarizing what you have said or by reinforcing your purpose statement. The conclusion is important because it may be the thing that the audience is most likely to remember. As evidence for this claim, most people remember Patrick Henry's concluding words, "Give me liberty or give me death," even if they do not remember the rest of his speech given in the Virginia Convention in 1775.

When it comes to the speech you are preparing, remember that you have to *plan* what you are going to say in the conclusion. Don't expect the right words to come to you in a moment of inspiration. Think about how you are going to end the speech, and write it on the outline pretty much the way you plan to say it.

The summary. If your speech is fairly long and contains detailed and complex material, you might want to end with a summary of the general ideas. This is a good practice when it is important that the audience be able to remember what you have said. Be careful, however, that your conclusion is not too redundant to the speech itself.

Reinforcement of the thesis. When you have a short speech, it might be a better idea simply to paraphrase your thesis as a means of reinforcing your main idea. Be sure that your conclusion is consistent with the thesis. I have heard speakers who have negated the effectiveness of their presentation by using words in the conclusion that seemed to contradict what they said in the body of the speech. It's very important that you have a clear understanding yourself of what it is that you want to reinforce.

Quotation. An effective way to conclude a speech is to use a quotation. This works well for two reasons: first, because the quote you selected will probably be pithy or clever or have emotional impact, and secondly, because you are bolstering your own credibility with the words of someone else who supports the point you want to make. To quote Brendan Francis, "A quotation in a speech, article, or book is like a rifle in the hands of an infantryman. It speaks with authority."

Here is a sample outline containing all the elements that have been described: the attention statement, the purpose statement, the presummary, the main headings, the supporting information, and the conclusion.

INTRODUCTION

Attention Statement: At one time the typical American family consisted of a mother, a father and 2.3 children. That description—with the father being the breadwinner and the mother staying home with the kids—actually represents a relatively small percentage of American families.

Purpose Statement: A great many single parents in the United States are struggling to rear their children alone and often are in need of welfare assistance. Today I would like to describe to you

- The extent of the problem
- The financial needs of single parents
- Some alternatives that might work better than what we are doing

BODY

I The problem of single-parent families has increased significantly in recent years.
   A The high divorce rate accounts for a large part of the problem.
      1 Over half of all marriages end in divorce.
      2 Three and a half million families are headed by women alone.
   B Absence of marriage is also a contributing factor.
      1 One out of every five children will be born to unwed parents.
      2 If the mother keeps the child, she generally rears it alone.

C The problem is more severe among blacks than among whites.
   1 87% of black children live in mother-only families.
   2 45% of white children are reared by mothers only.
II Single parents generally lose income and often face poverty unless they receive welfare.
   A Half of all single-parent families are below the poverty level.
      1 Average income is from $10,000 to $14,000.
      2 85% of that goes to cover rent and child care.
   B Aid to Families with Dependent Children
      1 Federal funds administered by county governments.
      2 85% of AFDC money goes to single parents.
   C Only one in five AFDC recipients receives support from absent parent.
      1 Often whereabouts of father is not known.
      2 Collection is difficult when state boundaries are crossed.
   D Women on AFDC tend to remain on it for an extended period of time.
      1 65% remain for eight years or longer.
      2 28% stay for only three to seven years.
      3 Only 7% get off in one or two years.
III State and local programs may work better than federal assistance.
   A Programs administered by state governments.
      1 Wisconsin's plan for holding absent parents responsible.
         a Child support payments automatically deducted from paycheck.
         b Plan has saved the state $50 million in welfare costs.
      2 Texas plan for keeping pregnant teenagers in school.
         a Provides child care on site.
         b 72% of teen mothers in Fort Worth graduate from high school; only 50%, before the program started.
   B Privately funded programs.
      1 HOME—Helping Ourselves Means Education.
         a Founded by Carol Sasaki, herself a former single parent on welfare.
         b Allows women to go to college; receive grants, loans, work-study funds.
         c Day care for children.
         d 11,000 women have been through the program.

CONCLUSION

We need to recognize that there are a great many single parents who need help. We certainly should do everything we can to require that absent parents take their share of the financial responsibility, but we must accept the fact that public and private assistance is also necessary.

THE FINISHED OUTLINE

By this time you have filled up all the boxes that were illustrated at the start of this chapter—you have the introduction, the body, and the conclusion. Now you can write the outline in its finished form and begin going over it; you want to be sure that it says what you want it to say, and that you are familiar with all the material. The outline is not complete until you are absolutely sure that the arrangement you have established is the way you want it to be. Read through the material out loud; listen to how the ideas are expressed, and make your own critical evaluation of the organizational structure. If changes are needed, make them at the preparation stage; don't do it spontaneously at the time of delivery. *Plan the speech you want to give, and give the speech you plan.*

EXERCISE

Select any speech from the periodical *Vital Speeches*, and analyze its organizational structure by answering the following questions:

- What did the speaker say to gain the audience's attention?
- What did the speaker say to establish the main purpose of the speech?
- What are three main ideas developed in the body of the speech?
- What is the most significant piece of evidence presented by the speaker?
- What did the speaker say to bring the speech to a conclusion?

QUESTIONS FOR REVIEW

1 What was the significant change in American industry that occurred in 1956?

2 What are three reasons that good organization is essential in public speaking?

3 What are the three basic structural elements of a speech outline?

4 What are the two important functions of the introduction?

5 What are the attention-getting devices that can be used at the start of the speech?

6 How does a rhetorical question differ from a response question?

7 What is meant by a *presummary*? What is the purpose of it?

8 What are you doing when you qualify the purpose statement?

9 What are you doing when you focus the topic?

10 Why should you keep the purpose statement in the back of your mind while you deliver the speech?

11 What is the function of the main heading in the outline?

12 Name four patterns for organizing the main headings in an outline.

13 What is the conclusion of the speech designed to do?

14 Why is a quotation often a good way to end a speech?

CHAPTER 5

THINKING AND REASONING

Whether the purpose of your speech is to inform or to convince, the conclusions you ask people to accept should only be those that you have thoughtfully considered. Presentations that are of real value to an audience are not the clever platitudes of a glib stage personality, but the intelligent deliberations of a person who is well informed and has a sincere commitment to the topic and to the interests of the listeners.

An important part of your preparation in public speaking is having a genuine desire to learn. You must develop the ability to recognize the significance of the information you hear and read, interpret its meaning, file it away in your mind, and retrieve it when you need it. The most effective speakers are those who have a good grasp of what they believe. They are well informed and are able to organize their thoughts when the occasion demands. As you develop the skills of public address, you will also be training your mind to think critically. You will learn to approach problems in a logical fashion, to evaluate your data, correct for error, and avoid jumping to irrational conclusions. These are important qualities for you to have, because ideas must make sense to you before you will be able to express them persuasively to anyone else.

CRITICAL THINKING

The term *critical thinking* refers to our ability to go beyond mere rote learning. Formal education often teaches facts without regard for developing the student's capacity to analyze, interpret, challenge, and see the implications and consequences of the data. If we are going to be able to write and speak intelligently, we need to be able to think critically. Richard Paul sees this as being an essential part of our education:

> What we say or write . . . is only a small portion of the thinking process—the proverbial tip of the iceberg. Surrounding any line of thought is a large substructure of *background thought,* logical connections not lying on the surface of reasoning, but prior to it, underlying it, or implied by it. In the background of all thinking are foundational concepts, assumptions, values, purposes, experiences, implications, and consequences—all embedded in lines of thought radiating outward in every direction.[1]

What this theory suggests is that the roots of public speaking go deep into the cerebral processes, and you are not going to be able to make substantive changes in your rhetorical skills merely by learning methods and techniques of oral delivery.

Selective Learning

First of all we must understand that what we learn goes through a selection process. We cannot possibly assimilate all the information that we are exposed to, so we open our minds to that which seems to be useful to us and close our minds to the rest. Even data we have mentally processed are not always retrievable, so we are limited to what we can recall or rediscover through experience or research. We can expect that our information is always going to be incomplete; what we would like to know may be unavailable to us, or it may not yet have been discovered by science. No matter how hard we try, we will never know it all. Nevertheless, we must make evaluations and judgments based on the best information we have.

Examining Beliefs

By the time you become an adult, your brain is full of information; some of it is accurate, and some is inaccurate. That which you believe to be true is what you call "reality," but it may be simply a belief pattern and not resemble the real world at all. For example, the "reality" of a man who believes that women biologically are not capable of understanding principles of finance is quite different from the "reality" of a woman who knows she has a talent for such work. Even though facts and evidence do not support his conclusion, the man will be inclined to act upon what he believes to be

[1] Richard Paul, *Critical Thinking,* Center for Critical Thinking and Moral Critique, Sonoma State University, Rohnert Park, Calif., 1990, p. 70.

What we learn and choose to accept goes through a selection process.

true. Since reality forms the basis of our behavior, such a man would probably not hire a woman to be his budget director regardless of what qualifications she may have. Thinking critically means we can learn to avoid making these kinds of irrational mistakes that adversely affect our lives and the lives of those around us.

Direct Experience   Some of our information comes to us by direct experience. We perceive it through one or more of our five senses—hearing, seeing, touching, tasting, and smelling. Knowledge we experience directly has more impact on us than that which we receive indirectly. It is also more apt to affect our thinking and will be retained for a longer period of time. For example, being in an automobile accident would surely have a profound effect on the way you think about traffic safety. Being witness to an accident would probably also make a strong impression. Other forms of learning, such as seeing a film, hearing a lecture, or reading an account, may in some degree influence your thinking, but not nearly so much as the direct experience.

Influence of Other People   While direct experience may be the most powerful form of learning, it is not always possible, necessary, or even desirable to acquire knowledge firsthand. A great deal of what we believe to be true comes about as a result of information we receive from other people. As small children, we learn from parents, siblings, peers, and perhaps eccentric relatives; later in life we also learn from books, teachers, and the mass media. Because our information comes to us from such a variety of sources, we can assume that a certain portion of it will be inaccurate, biased, or misleading. The quality we call "wisdom" depends to a large extent on our ability to perceive the difference between information that is valid and that which is faulty.

Testing What You Hear and Read

Some reports you hear and read in the mass media are more reliable than others, and if you are to base your beliefs on what appears in newspapers and on television, you must have some way of knowing whether or not you can trust the source. The validity of published and broadcast material can be tested by asking the following questions:

1 Is the source reputable? Has other information from the same source been found to be accurate?

2 Does the source have any obvious bias? Is it a publication financed by an organization in support of one side or the other of an issue?

3 Has the source provided complete information, or have important parts been left out? Have quotations been taken out of context? Would the rest of the context change the meaning?

4 Has the source given the most current information? Have later events changed the circumstances?

5 Does the information meet the test of reason, or are there internal inconsistencies? Does the information contradict something else you know to be true?

6 Do other sources corroborate the information? If so, are those other sources reliable? Are there reasons why one source would possess facts others do not have?

7 Is the language of the source objective? Does the information contain emotionally loaded terminology designed solely for the purpose of arousing fear or hatred? Is the source attempting to discredit a person or a cause with diatribe rather than reason?

Be suspicious of sources that do not meet these criteria. If you are not sure that the information is accurate, seek verification. If you find that you have been misinformed and have arrived at conclusions based on erroneous data, don't hesitate to make corrections in your thinking.

Learning What You Need to Know

By itself, memorizing words, theories, and facts is not a path that leads to critical thought. However, you cannot test data and draw conclusions unless you have a foundation of knowledge to use as a starting point. You can argue that there is no need to learn a lot of big words and commit facts to memory so long as you know where to find the information and the terminology when you need it. That's true to a certain extent, but without having some fundamental background, you won't be aware of what specific words, theories, or evidence you will need to find.

Vocabulary   Words and their definitions are important, not just for the sake of expressing ideas, but for thinking about them. For example, a person who is *environmentally anthropocentric* is one who promotes the preservation of nature, not because of a sentimental concern for the life of other creatures, but for the survival of humankind. The thesis, of course, is more important than the terminology, but having a broad vocabulary makes it possible for you to consider a greater variety of notions. Memorizing words and definitions out of a dictionary certainly will not contribute to your capacity for critical thought, but reflecting on the implications of new terminology will expand the horizons of your thinking.

A good dictionary is an important resource for a public speaker. If possible, use one that is large enough to offer more than a single definition. Notice that in the above example the word *anthropocentric* is used in a way that pertains to environmental concerns; it can have different meanings if it is applied to religion, psychology, or sociology. For this reason we need to consider that building a broad and effective vocabulary is not likely to happen if we try to do it one word at a time. Words have limited value unless they are used in context, so we must learn to recognize the significance of their meaning in relationship to other words. Vocabulary is important to our intellectual growth not only as a means of expanding our thought, but also as a vehicle to express what we want to say. In order to convey ideas the way we intend for them to be received, we must be able to select words that accurately say what we mean.

Literary References   Communicating effectively requires more than just having a broad vocabulary and knowing the meaning of a lot of words. It is also incumbent upon a speaker to be familiar with the historical and literary references that are common to the culture. In his book *Cultural Literacy*, E. D. Hirsch says, "To understand what somebody is saying, we must understand more than just the surface meaning of the words; we have to understand the context as well."[2] Hirsch refers to a test given to a group of community college students that was designed to measure reading comprehension. A passage in the text included reference to the meeting of Ulysses S. Grant and Robert E. Lee in the parlor of the Appomattox Courthouse on April 9, 1865. While the students knew the meaning of all the words in the passage, many of them failed to grasp the gist of the story because they did not connect the facts to the U.S. Civil War. That background knowledge may be important if the subject matter of your speech deals with anything that has to do with affirmative action, integration in schools, equal opportunity in employment, or the rights of states versus the rights of the federal government.

Not knowing about the events of the Civil War or the reasons why Robert E. Lee chose to fight on the side of the south makes it difficult to understand the significance of the 1954 Supreme Court decision in *Brown v. the Topeka Board of Education* or the Civil Rights Act of 1964. How does all of this relate to what a speaker needs to do to prepare to meet the audience? Thinking people (and those are the ones whom you must be prepared to address when you study speech at the college level) will expect you to have some understanding of the history, politics, socioeconomic structure, art, and science that form the basis for the values of the society. If your subject matter pertains in any way to events or concepts that are regarded as common knowledge within the culture, you are not fully prepared unless you have at least some awareness of them.

Interpreting Information and Drawing Conclusions

Educators continually strive to find the most effective mix of pedagogical methods that will stimulate the critical thinking process. Do students need to learn facts? Certainly they do; otherwise they will believe that everything is simply a matter of opinion. Do they need to learn how to interpret information and draw conclusions? Absolutely. If our schools rely totally on rote learning, they are engaged in a conditioning process rather than education.

Thinking critically is difficult and is frequently rejected in favor of easier and less taxing methods of reaching conclusions. All too often peo-

[2] E. D. Hirsch, Jr., *Cultural Literacy,* Houghton Mifflin, Boston, 1987, p. 3.

Avoid restricting your thinking to "bumper sticker mentality."

ple rely on platitudes or simplistic slogans—a thought process that might be called "bumper sticker mentality." This is a term that refers to applying some cleverly phrased statement to an issue without analyzing the meaning of the words or their validity in a given situation. The man in the earlier example who had a fixed belief about women and the principles of finance may have drawn his conclusion from the expression "A woman's place is in the home." Such a statement is not based on evidence or reason but on mindless repetition. The problem is that we tend to listen to people without making a critical evaluation of what we hear.

CRITICAL LISTENING AND FALLACIES IN LOGIC

We can learn a lot when we listen, so long as we listen with a critical ear. It is not enough just to absorb information; we must also be prepared to analyze it and determine whether or not it makes sense. Are we willing to accept the whole message or only part of it? What kind of response do we want to make? Should we affirm or refute what is said? Critical listening is especially important in a political setting. Our ability to process information given to us by a candidate for office is vital in order for a democracy to function. Year after year public officials are returned to office by voters who may have heard the voices of the candidates but did not listen critically to their arguments and reasoning.

Cleverness is not a substitute for substance. There are a number of rhetorical devices that can be used by a speaker to gain and hold attention, but they do little or nothing to contribute to understanding. Catchy phrases and humorous anecdotes make a speech appealing to listen to and are certainly not to be condemned. But as a discerning listener, you may want to ask yourself, "Is the speaker using clever rhetoric to cover up a lack of substance or to avoid confronting the issue directly?" Look for the smoke screens that are designed to conceal rather than illuminate the speaker's meaning. There are several well-known devices called *fallacies in logic.*[3]

A **red herring** is a diversionary tactic designed to prejudice the issue under consideration by relating it to a common fear. It is employed for the sole purpose of alarming the audience by claiming an improbable consequence that is only remotely connected to the issue. *Example:* People who oppose gun control in any form sometimes use the argument that if registration of firearms is required, the government will know where all the weapons are; then agents would be able to go around the country and confiscate them all so that citizens would have no way of defending themselves. *Analysis:* Disarming the population is a red herring because there are other reasons for gun registration that have nothing to do with confiscating weapons. It is highly unlikely that in a democratic nation such as ours the government would ever need to become that hostile to the population.

A **straw man** strategy diverts attention away from the opposition's strong arguments to ones that can easily be attacked. *Example:* Debaters who argue against capital punishment will try to make it seem as though the main reason people have for wanting to execute criminals is to get revenge. *Analysis:* While some supporters of capital punishment are motivated by the desire for vengeance, the stronger arguments, and the ones that need to be addressed, are those which deal with deterring thieves from carrying weapons during a robbery, protecting prison guards from inmates who have nothing to lose, and making it impossible for the criminal to return to society and commit further crimes.

An ***ad populum*** argument appeals to what a speaker knows to be the existing prejudices of the audience. *Example:* Hitler relied heavily on *ad populum* arguments in his diatribes against the Jews and the Bolsheviks

---

[3] For a more complete list see Joe Ayres and Janice Miller, *Effective Public Speaking,* Brown, Dubuque, Iowa, 1983, pp. 227–228.

because he knew that fear and hatred of those groups already existed in the minds of his listeners. In our own country before the Civil Rights Act, politicians in the southern states commonly loaded their speeches with racist remarks because they knew that was the way to appeal to their constituents on a feeling level. In fact, few candidates were able to get elected unless they clearly supported segregation. *Analysis:* When speakers use prejudice as a ploy to gain favor, they are exploiting the audience's weaknesses and are denying them exposure to rational arguments. Another word for this ploy is *demagoguery.*

An **ad hominem** strategy attempts to win a debate by making unsupported accusations to discredit an adversary's integrity rather than by confronting the person's arguments with real refutation. In the political arena, this tactic is referred to as "name calling." *Example:* A speaker attacks the opposing candidate by saying he is unqualified to make decisions because he is a drunkard. *Analysis:* Terminology of this kind is meaningless because it is entirely subjective. The person in question might simply be a social drinker by the standards of other people. The speaker is saying more about his or her own animosity than about the qualifications of the opponent.

Begging the question asks the audience to accept a premise as though it were a foregone conclusion without offering supporting evidence. *Example:* A speaker says, "Everyone knows, of course, that if the generals had been allowed to do their job, we could have won the war in Vietnam." *Analysis:* "Everyone" does not know that to be the case. The speaker is trying to make it seem as though the statement is not controversial when it is, in fact, highly argumentative. The point would have to be advanced as a thesis or a claim and be supported with reasons. It is not an assumption that can be accepted at face value.

A **circular argument** is one in which the line of reasoning returns to the thesis as being its own proof. *Example:* Marijuana should not be legalized because it is harmful. The reason it is harmful is that if people get caught selling it, they will go to jail. *Analysis:* A thesis must be proved with reasons outside itself; otherwise, the arguer is simply repeating what has already been said.

Non sequitur literally means "not in sequence." In other words, a statement does not follow in a logical sequence from the previous one. *Example:* A parent says to a child, "Of course you have to go to college; your grandfather could never afford a new suit." *Analysis:* There may be a connection in the mind of the parent, but the message is confusing to the receiver who might not see the relationship between the two statements.

Post hoc ergo propter hoc is a Latin phrase for "after this, therefore because of this." The fallacy of this reasoning is based on the claim that because one event follows another, the first was the cause of the second. *Ex-*

ample: People who live along the San Andreas fault in California try very hard to figure out when earthquakes will occur. Some projections are based on the weather, others on alignment of the planets. The reasoning is that because certain conditions existed just before previous earthquakes, there is a cause-and-effect relationship. *Analysis:* We cannot know whether one event is the cause of another unless we conduct a scientifically controlled study. Making a casual observation is generally not a reliable basis for forming a realistic belief. As listeners, we have a right to require more substantial evidence.

Critical listening is closely related to critical thinking. The arguments we hear expressed by other people are often incorporated into our own way of reasoning. In a complex society such as ours we are bombarded continuously by a barrage of words that urge us to buy, sell, vote, and behave in a variety of ways. We are exposed to more information than we can possibly process—some of it valuable, much of it useless or counterproductive. If we accept that which is illogical and laden with fallacies, our own thought and discourse will become equally contaminated. We must learn to be selective in what we accept as truth and base our conclusions on evidence rather than unsupported assertions.

THE INDUCTIVE PROCESS

One way we can arrive at a reasoned conclusion is by using a method called the *inductive process.* We sometimes refer to this as the *scientific method* because conclusions are deferred until the evidence has been gathered. As part of this process you may start by forming a *hypothesis.* That means you make a guess about what the conclusion might be, but you do not rely on it until you have examined the data. For example, the man who believed that women were not capable of comprehending principles of finance might have reached a different conclusion if he had first considered the facts:

1 Standardized tests indicate that women score just as high as men on instruments that measure quantitative reasoning.
2 Colleges and universities report no difference in grade point averages between men and women in classes dealing with financial matters.
3 Women who have pursued careers in finance have performed just as successfully as men. Indeed, women have served as treasurer of the United States in several different administrations.

All these data conflict with the hypothesis; consequently, the man mentioned earlier would have to alter his conclusion and acknowledge that a woman could be just as good a budget director as a man. When you follow this procedure, you are using the inductive method of reasoning—allowing the evidence to lead you to a conclusion rather than accepting a notion because of previous beliefs.

The scientific method works the same way. When a study is conducted, researchers set up a series of experiments, being careful to control the variable factors. They will then make an alteration in the condition to be studied; for example, varying the diet of laboratory rats. After observing the results, they will form a hypothesis and conduct the study again. If the same results occur each time the experiment is performed, and if the researchers are able to predict each time what the outcome will be, they are able to say that the study has reliability. If the results are consistent with other studies of the same nature, a conclusion can be drawn that there is a cause-and-effect relationship.

Signs and Causes

All too frequently we tend to draw conclusions on the basis of insufficient evidence. If several of our friends lose their jobs, for example, we might be tempted to say that the country is in a recession. Certainly the loss of a few jobs is not sufficient reason to form a generalization. If we look at nation-wide statistics, however, we might get a better indication. When unemployment figures climb to 6 or 7 percent, we might be able to say that a recession is occurring, but still we are basing our conclusion on just one index. There is other evidence we need in order to support a declaration concerning the economic health of the nation. We would look at the gross domestic product, the balance of trade, and perhaps the number of new housing construction starts. If all the evidence is consistent with our hypothesis, we might be able to see a pattern. Even then, we need to recognize that in a subject area as complex as the economic conditions of the nation, the claims we make are going to be based on values as well as quantitative evidence.

Data we use to form a belief that a problem exists are called *signs*. We must be careful not to confuse signs with *causes*. Sometimes the language we use distorts the logical progression of our thoughts. We might say, "The nation is in a recession because the unemployment rate has risen to 7 percent." We don't mean that the high unemployment rate has *caused* the recession; we mean that the 7 percent rate is a *sign* that a recession exists. It is for this reason that we need to study the use of language simultaneously with examining the processes we use in interpreting data and forming conclusions. We must be able to speak clearly and logically to ourselves as well as to other people.

THE DEDUCTIVE PROCESS

When we are reasoning through the inductive process, we don't begin with a premise or a generalization; we begin with specific evidence and then follow it to see where it leads. This is why we say that inductive reasoning proceeds from specific information to a general conclusion. When we reason *deductively,* we start with a general principle that we believe to be true and apply it to a particular situation. You may read, for example, about Sherlock Holmes noticing a bit of red mud on the boot of a suspect and concluding that the person has been walking through the moors. That's when Dr. Watson says, "Brilliant deduction, Holmes." The master detective is using what we call *syllogistic* reasoning, which is constructed in the following manner:

> Red mud can be picked up on a boot only by walking through the moors.
> That man has red mud on his boot.
> That man has been walking through the moors.

Holmes would probably reply, "Elementary, my dear Watson." Indeed it does appear to be elementary; however, it is the *method* of reasoning that we want to examine.

A *syllogism* is a rhetorical device that can be used to analyze the validity of a conclusion. We won't go too deeply into the rules for syllogisms because they can get very complex; all we need at this time is to have a basic understanding of the theory behind them. A categorical syllogism has three parts:

- A major premise that must be accepted as an unqualified truth
- A minor premise that is a specific case governed by the major premise
- A conclusion

The classic example is as follows:

- All men are mortal. (Major premise.)
- John is a man. (Minor premise.)
- John is mortal. (Conclusion.)

If the major premise is true, and if the minor premise is governed by it, the conclusion must *necessarily* be accepted. Be sure to note, however, that both the major premise and the minor premise are subject to refutation. If you wanted to reject a conclusion drawn from syllogistic reasoning, you would have to demonstrate either that the major premise was not true or that the minor premise was not governed by it. To challenge Sherlock Holmes' reasoning, you might argue that red mud could be picked up somewhere else other than on the moors, or that the boots had been worn by some other person.

It's not just in detective work that we find applications for syllogistic reasoning. The syllogism is a rhetorical tool that can be used whenever you want to argue that a specific example is or should be included in the category of a major premise. It can become a way of making the social system work for you.

- All children are entitled to an education.
- Jane is a child.
- Jane is entitled to an education.

So long as there are no exceptions to the major premise, and so long as Jane (minor premise) is included in the category of all children (major premise), the conclusion must logically be accepted.

The logic of a syllogism seems easy enough to understand, but sometimes the point of view we hold gets in the way of our being able to recognize it. Suppose you are a young man and your father says to you, "No, son, you can't have the car tonight. I've been reading insurance reports on male drivers between the ages of 18 and 25. There's no question about it. Young men in that age bracket are unsafe drivers, and since you are 19, that includes you." Does Dad have a valid syllogism? As a matter of fact, he does.

- All young men between 18 and 25 are unsafe drivers.
- You are a young man between 18 and 25.
- Therefore, you are an unsafe driver.

Does this mean he wins the argument? Not at all. You can't attack his logic, but you can challenge his major premise. It's not true that *all* young men between 18 and 25 are unsafe drivers; even the insurance reports would not say that. He might be able to claim that *most* of them are unsafe, but once he changes his major premise, his syllogism is no longer valid. At that point you can attack his logic and get the car (provided Dad is a reasonable person).

The *rule of law* provides us with another example of where syllogistic reasoning can be applied. We say in this country that all people are equal under the law. That means that everyone is entitled to due process of the law; it also means that the penalties must be applied equally. The law, then, can be used as the major premise in a syllogism:

- All people using a gun in committing a crime must go to jail.
- The defendant used a gun holding up a liquor store.
- The defendant must go to jail.

This example leads us to an important principle of our social structure. If we are to have a fair system of justice, the rules of law must be based on reason rather than the inclination of judges. In this country we say that a person is innocent until proved guilty, and that the burden of proof is on the prosecutor rather than the defendant. Even before a case is allowed to come to trial, the district attorney must be able to satisfy a judge that there is evidence against the person charged. Then, the prosecutor must be able to present a prima facie case in order to get a conviction.

A *Prima Facie* Case

A *prima facie* case is one which is constructed in such a way that the conclusion must necessarily be accepted unless one or more of the major contentions is rejected. Normally, the prosecuting attorney would begin the trial by presenting to the jury an outline of the case that the state has against the defendant. If the charge is armed robbery, the following claims would have to be proved:

- That a robbery was committed
- That the defendant was the one who committed the robbery
- That the defendant carried a firearm at the time of the robbery

The next step would be for the prosecutor to support all three of those claims with evidence. If the jury members believed all of them to be true, they would have to return a verdict of guilty. And if the law were to be upheld, the defendant would have to go to jail. In order to discredit the case, the defense attorney would have to successfully refute the evidence that supports one or more of the main contentions.

As you can see, there is a similarity between the prima facie case and the syllogism. In both circumstances the conclusion must necessarily be accepted unless the opposition is successful in demonstrating that one or more of the main contentions is not true.

FRAMEWORK FOR PROBLEM SOLVING

Every time we pick up the newspaper, we read about problems that need solutions. The word *problem* need not be regarded as a synonym for *trouble*. We are imperfect people living in an imperfect society, and problems are part of our everyday life. We can look at problems in several different ways: We can ignore them and pretend they don't exist; we can worry about them and do nothing; or we can confront them and find solutions. The last choice seems to be the most sensible as long as we use effective methods in dealing with them. Sometimes our gut-level response works all

Begin the reflective thinking process by defining and limiting the scope of the problem.

right, but when issues are complex, we may need to rely on a more rational approach.

The philosopher and educator John Dewey has given us a method called the *reflective thinking process.*[4] It has been adapted in a number of ways to a variety of situations, but here is the basic framework:

- **Define the problem.** State the problem in a way that clearly identifies it. If you can't put it into words, you probably don't really understand what it is.

- **Limit the problem.** Bring the problem into focus so that it is distinguished from other issues. The more you are able to pinpoint the problem, the better chance you will have to find a solution.

- **Analyze the data.** This step consists of gathering information that is related to the problem. Your data may suggest how the problem developed, how serious it is, and what effect it is having.

[4] John Dewey, *How We Think,* Heath, Boston, 1933, pp. 106–115.

- **Establish criteria for solutions.** Before you decide on a solution, you need to have some idea of what you want the solution to achieve.
- **Consider possible solutions.** Here you have a chance to think creatively. Don't get locked into believing that there is only one answer to a problem; open your mind to more possibilities.
- **Select the best solution by checking each possibility against your criteria.** Consider all the alternatives in light of what you said you wanted your solution to accomplish; then pick the one that fits best.

This framework can be a useful tool in dealing with complex problems, but remember that you have to be realistic. There is no such thing as a perfect solution.

Thinking Through a Problem

To illustrate the problem-solving framework, let's look at the issue of street drugs. Everybody has an opinion on how to deal with this problem, but often the conclusion people reach is based on oversimplified thinking that doesn't take into consideration the complexities of the issue. Don't make the mistake of making a speech on a topic like this before you have pursued in your mind a logical progression of thought.

Define the Problem   Begin by identifying in a general sense what you perceive the problem to be. Do you want to address the debilitating effects that drugs have on the individual, or are you more concerned about the damaging consequences to society? A broad definition of the topic might be simply that the sale and use of street drugs in the United States appears to be a serious social problem.

Limit the Topic   Once you have the general idea, you can begin thinking about how to limit the topic. The scope of the problem as stated is too extensive for you to handle in one study, so you will have to be more specific in order to make an effective report. The limitations you put on the topic might be in terms of the particular drugs and the specific segments of the society that are affected. For example, you might sharpen the focus of the topic by posing the question in the following way: How extensive is the sale and use of crack cocaine in the public schools, and what methods work best to deal with the problem?

Analyze the Data   Begin by doing some reading on the subject, and talk to people who are informed on the topic. You may also want to structure your research by posing a list of questions:

- What effect does crack cocaine have on the people who use it?
- How much does it cost, and how do students get the money to buy it?
- How many students use the drug, and how old are they when they start?
- What motivates students to begin using crack cocaine?
- How much crime is related to drug trafficking?
- What role do students play in the gangs that supply the drug?
- Where does the drug come from? How does it get into the country and into the schools?
- What effect does the drug problem have on the quality of education?
- What are school officials doing to curtail the use of drugs?
- What happens to a student who is caught using or selling drugs?
- What are the courts and the law enforcement officials doing about the problem?

You may not be able to find answers to all these questions, but at least the list will help you to think about what you need to know and what the audience might ask.

Establish Criteria for the Solution This is an important step and one that is too often left out. It is a hard step to take because it requires insight, judgment, and objective thinking. What frequently happens is that solutions come to mind while you are analyzing the data. Those solutions may appear to be very attractive, and you might be tempted to start right away to build a case in their support. Before you do this, however, consider what goals you want your solution to accomplish. Here are six possible criteria:

1 Significantly reduce the sale and distribution of crack cocaine in public schools.

2 Modify the attitude of students so that they are not motivated to try drugs.

3 Improve the learning environment for students.

4 Provide rehabilitation for those addicted to drugs.

5 Punish the offenders and prevent them from repeating their crime.

6 Provide a means for students to earn money without having to sell drugs.

Some of these criteria may be more important than others, and you will have to decide which ones you want to focus on in this particular study.

Consider Possible Solutions Now you are ready to start thinking about possible ways to solve the problem. This step in the process calls for creative thinking as well as critical thinking. You very likely will find that complex social problems are much easier to describe than they are to solve. Open your mind to possibilities, and get them down on paper. Your list might look something like this:

A Developing support programs and rehabilitation centers for students who want to quit the drug habit

B Giving special privileges to students who stay off drugs

C Providing job opportunities for students who would otherwise be selling drugs

D Closing the campus so that no one is allowed in or out until school is over

E Requiring that students who are caught using drugs attend school in separate facilities

F Prosecuting students in adult courts when they are caught selling drugs

Select the Best Solution   The way to select the best solution is to measure each one of them against your criteria and see which one comes the closest to accomplishing what you want to have happen. In addition to producing the most effective solution, this method also gives you one that is defensible; you will be able to explain why the solution you selected was chosen over the other possibilities. This is an important feature of the method because it is quite likely that you will be called upon to do precisely that.

DISCOVERING WHAT YOU BELIEVE

After you have gone through all the steps in the framework for problem solving, you will be ready to begin putting together a speech to convince. Be realistic about what you are able to accomplish, and limit the number of recommendations you advocate. One of the benefits of a speech course is that the student often develops an appreciation for those who have the responsibility for inventing and implementing solutions. Lawmakers, administrators, and people in positions of authority have a more difficult job than we sometimes believe—they have to take into consideration a great many consequences that may result from the policies they establish.

Be as specific as you can be in making your recommendations. You may propose to your audience that people learn to protect the environment, or fight to preserve their freedoms, but such assertions have no functional application. It isn't hard to get people to see the value of some abstract virtue; disagreement occurs when you begin to talk about details. For example, you may be saying in your speech that unnecessary expenses must be cut; this is a statement with which every person in your audience might thoroughly agree. But if you are forced to be specific about where those cuts should come, you are likely to confront opposition. Do not expect unanimous approval. Whenever you make specific declarations on a controversial issue, you are bound to gain the support of some and lose the support of others.

The process of discovering what you believe is sometimes referred to as *dialectical thinking.* Richard Paul says:

> Whenever we consider concepts or issues deeply, we naturally explore their connections to other ideas and issues within different domains or points of view. Court trials and debates are dialectical in form and intention. They pit idea against idea, reasoning against counterreasoning in order to get at the truth of a matter. As soon as we begin to explore ideas, we find that some clash or are inconsistent with others. If we are to integrate our thinking, we need to assess which of the conflicting ideas we will accept . . .[5]

There is some risk involved in this practice, because the evidence and the logical thought process may lead you to a conclusion that you don't really want to accept. Oliver Wendell Holmes said, "What is true is what I can't help believing." Being in that position may make you feel uncomfortable at first, but it will also make you a better and a more reasonable public speaker.

EXERCISE

Review the steps in the "framework for problem solving" and the issue of the sale and use of street drugs in public schools. Note that there are six choices under the heading of "establishing criteria for the solution." There are also six choices under the heading of "possible solutions." For each criterion there is a corresponding solution, and your task is to match the ones that go together. Remember that when you develop a speech on an issue of this kind, the solution you advocate must correspond to the problem you have described.

QUESTIONS FOR REVIEW

1 What do we mean by *critical thinking?*
2 What do we mean by *selective learning?*
3 Which has more impact on us, direct experience or reports we read? Why?

---

[5] Richard Paul, op. cit., p. 254.

4 What are questions we should ask in order to test the validity of sources?

5 Why is vocabulary important in both the thinking and the speaking process?

6 What does Hirsch mean by *cultural literacy?* How can it affect our understanding of messages?

7 In order to become educated people what do we have to do in addition to learning facts?

8 What is meant by a *red herring? A straw man?*

9 What is the difference between *ad populum* and *ad hominem?*

10 What is a circular argument? A non sequitur? *Post hoc ergo propter hoc?*

11 What is another term for inductive reasoning? Describe how the process works.

12 What is the difference between a sign and a cause?

13 What are we doing when we reason deductively?

14 What are the three parts of a categorical syllogism?

15 What do you have to do before you can logically reject the conclusion of a syllogism?

16 How can a syllogism be applied to the rule of law?

17 In what way is a syllogism similar to a prima facie case?

18 What are the steps in the problem-solving framework?

CHAPTER 6

THE SPEECH TO CONVINCE

You might say that every speech you prepare is designed to convince in one way or another. You want to convince your audience that you are a credible person, that your information is accurate, and that your message has significant value. In terms of rhetorical categories, however, the *speech to convince* is usually thought of as one that deals with a controversial topic. When you prepare for this kind of speech, you must assume that there will be people in the audience who will be opposed to your thesis; you want to persuade them to reevaluate their thinking and accept what you want them to believe.

THE PERSUASIVE MESSAGE

Before going any deeper into this subject, reflect a bit on how you feel about the term *persuasion.* You may be one of those who believes that persuading others is the same as trying to get them to do something they really don't want to do. "After all," you might ask, "what right do I have to tell people what they should believe or how they ought to behave?" You may also resent having someone try to persuade you to do something— particularly if you have had bad experiences with high-pressure salespeople. Even if the persuaders have your best interest at heart, you may object to their insistence on your doing things their way. And it doesn't reduce your irritation much when they tell you they are doing it "for your own good."

In order to discuss the art of persuasion intelligently, we must understand that in its pure classical or academic sense, it is neither coercive nor deceptive. If it were, its methods would certainly not find a proper place in a college textbook. The reason the term sometimes evokes a negative reaction is that it frequently is associated with practices that *are* designed to threaten or deceive. What we need to do is to qualify the definition of *persuasion* and show how it differs in nature from terms that appear to be similar.

Coercion is one way to get people to do what you want them to do. Here you are using force or the threat of force to get them to comply. It is different from persuasion in terms of the end result. People who are coerced may do what they are told to do for as long as the pressure is applied, but they will return to their former behavior when the threat is removed. They conform to your wishes, not because you have offered convincing evidence, but because they fear the consequences if they do not. Coercion is not persuasion; it is the exercise of power.

Manipulation is a devious tactic for getting what you want. It plays on emotional insecurities such as guilt, shame, fear, or sense of obligation. People who are manipulated may comply reluctantly, but they don't like themselves very much for having done so. An encyclopedia salesperson might say to a customer, "Now you don't want to deprive your children of all the educational advantages they deserve, do you?" This is not persuasion; it is a manipulative device designed to get a sale rather than to meet the needs of the customer. One way to understand the distinction between these terms is to see how they differ in regard to sexual relationships. Think of coercion as being analogous to rape, and manipulation as corresponding to seduction. Both of these are quite different from two people making love by mutual consent.[1]

Bribery is probably the easiest way to influence people, but here again we are employing an underhanded, rather than a persuasive, method. The person who accepts a bribe is making a choice based on personal gain rather than the merits of the proposal itself. To extend the sexual analogy we could say that bribery is a form of prostitution and is demeaning to both the giver and the receiver.

Deception is another device that can be used to change a person's belief or behavior, but deliberate falsehoods certainly have no place in the legitimate art of persuasion. *Deception* means distorting the facts or exaggerating the claims when you know that a true statement would not be convincing. This does not meet the definition of persuasion, because it denies

---

[1] Douglas Ehninger and Wayne Brockriede, *Decisions by Debate,* Harper & Row, New York, 1978, pp. 30–31.

recipients the chance to make a choice based on accurate information. When people find out they have been deceived, they will reject not only what you have told them, but also any further efforts you may make to try to influence them.

When we practice the art of persuasion, we are expressing what we honestly believe to be true. We are not trying to take advantage of our listeners—we want them to be the *beneficiaries* of our message, not the *victims.* We share with the audience the evidence, the reasons, and the logic that we, ourselves, have used in arriving at a conclusion. And we recognize that our listeners have free choice to accept or reject what we are saying. If we do anything that deprives them of that choice, we are using devious, rather than persuasive, methods.

MODES OF PROOF

Aristotle analyzed persuasion in terms of the elements that affect the people to whom the message is directed. He contended that those elements or modes were the logos, the pathos, and the ethos. These terms correspond roughly to the *argumentation,* the *emotional appeals,* and the *ethical qualities* that the speaker brings to the speech.

Logos

The term *logos* refers to the efforts the speaker is making to prove a case on the basis of facts and reason. If the controversial aspect of a speech can be addressed at the cognitive level, a speaker might be successful in changing the minds of the listeners by offering evidence that refutes what they have previously believed. A speech that is effective in this way is one which contains strong argumentation. When we speak of *argumentation,* we mean "the logical principles which underlie the examination and presentation of persuasive claims. . . . It is this focus on logical processes which distinguishes the study of argumentation from the study of persuasion."[2] In other words, persuasion is a broader term than argumentation. This may sound like a fine point of difference, but when you are sitting on a jury, it is important for you to know if the prosecutor is attempting to persuade you by appealing to your reason or to your emotions. Certainly emotional appeals are legitimate as a means of persuasion, but rhetorically they are not the same as the proofs that Aristotle calls the "logos."

---

[2]George W. Ziegelmueller and Charles A. Dause, *Argumentation, Inquiry and Advocacy,* Prentice Hall, Englewood Cliffs, N.J., 1975, p. 4.

Pathos

An appeal to the emotions is what we call the *pathos*. A speaker may be able to influence an audience by arousing their feelings of fear, anger, compassion, or sense of justice. Here again we can use the courtroom as an example. An attorney for a plaintiff in a personal injury suit would have to provide evidence (logos) to prove that an act of violence was committed, but the extent of suffering that was endured by the victim can only be measured on an emotional scale. The jury might agree that the defendant was responsible for the act, but differ in terms of their compassion for the offended party. The difference here might be quite real when it comes to the amount of damages awarded to the plaintiff. Recently the United States Supreme Court ruled that testimony pertaining to "victim impact" could be considered by juries in cases that involve the death penalty. This decision allows the punishment of a person convicted of a capital crime to be determined by emotional appeals.

While we certainly strive to be logical in what we say and do, a great many of the issues of our time are judged by emotion rather than by reason. We are called upon to make decisions based on whatever evidence is available, but we frequently find that facts are not enough. One of the most powerful speeches of this century is that which was delivered by Martin Luther King on August 28, 1963, from the steps of the Lincoln Memorial. In that address he said:

> I have a dream that my four little children will one day live in a nation where they will not be judged by the color of their skin, but by the content of their character.

Consider the influence these words had on civil rights legislation in this country. There is nothing here that could be called "factual evidence"; yet, people were profoundly moved by the power of the statement.

Ethos

Neither of the first two modes of proof mentioned so far—the logos or the pathos—would influence an audience unless the speaker displayed a sense of *ethos*. To use Aristotle's words, "There is persuasion through character whenever the speech is spoken in such a way as to make the speaker worthy of credence; for we believe fair-minded people to a greater extent and more quickly than we do others. . . ."[3] The evidence that is presented in a speech or the phrases that are used to create an emotional impact have a much greater effect on listeners who have confidence in the integrity of

---

[3] *Aristotle, On Rhetoric,* George A. Kennedy (trans.), Oxford University Press, New York, 1991, p. 38.

the speaker. Certainly, words themselves have influence of their own, but in order to explain why it is that Martin Luther King was able to achieve the success that he did, we have to look beyond the words and give credit to the persona of the speaker. It is unlikely that the same words spoken by someone else on the occasion of the 1963 civil rights rally would have had the same effect.

TELLING YOUR STORY

A speech to convince is generally thought of as one in which you advance argumentation. This is true much of the time, but not always. A speech on a controversial topic might consist simply of telling your story. Norma Mc-Corvey, an ordinary woman from a small town in Texas, is a person who found herself in just such a situation. She became a principal party in the abortion issue when she assumed the alias of Jane Roe and allowed her case to be brought before the United States Supreme Court. In 1973 the Court ruled in *Roe v. Wade* that having an abortion was a constitutional right for all women, and Norma McCorvey became the subject of nation-wide attention. When she speaks to an audience, she often begins by saying, "I am not a speaker; I'm a house painter." She does in fact make her living painting houses; she became a speaker, not because she wanted to, but because she had a story to tell.

The personal experiences in your life have a lot to do with the way you form your opinions on issues. That might suggest that people who have the same experiences form the same opinions. Not necessarily. A woman in the same situation as Norma McCorvey might come to an entirely differ-ent conclusion about abortion. The event alone is not what formulates your thinking; it's the way you perceive the event. You become persuasive when you are able to bring your audience around to seeing events in the same way that you do.

STATUS QUO

In any speech that involves argumentation, it is essential that you under-stand the prevailing conditions. The term *status quo* means "the way things are." It could refer to the laws that are in effect, the generally accepted standards of morality, or any other present state or condition. Your argu-mentative position will be either to support the status quo or to call for some modification of it.

Let's say that you want to give a speech to a group of concerned citizens who were interested in mass media. You have selected as your topic recent developments pertaining to the fairness doctrine. You would need to pro-vide orientation to your topic by explaining that the fairness doctrine was

Personal experiences have a lot to do with the way you form your opinions.

a policy which had, for many years, been used by the Federal Communications Commission (FCC) to see that radio and television stations did not restrict their editorializing to limited points of view. The rationale for this edict was that the airwaves belong to the public and broadcasters had a responsibility to see that fair consideration was given to all sides of controversial issues. The status quo changed in 1987 when the FCC ruled that the requirements of the fairness doctrine would no longer be imposed upon broadcasting stations. Having made this explanation, you could proceed to advance your arguments by either attacking or defending the status quo.

If you choose to attack the status quo, your responsibility is to describe what problem has been caused or will be caused as a result of the existing situation. In this case you might claim that removal of the restrictions of the fairness doctrine gives the big broadcasting stations an inordinate amount of power to influence public opinion according to their own bias. They are now at liberty to give airtime only to those people who support causes favored by the management.

On the other hand, when you defend the status quo, you are saying that the new ruling is necessary to preserve what we value. In this case you would argue that broadcasting stations should have the same right to editorialize as the newspapers and that depriving them of the right to program as they choose is suppressing freedom of speech. You could also make a case that restrictions imposed by the fairness doctrine formerly inhibited the discussion of controversial issues because radio and television stations were reluctant to air editorials of any kind, fearing that the FCC would require that equal time be made available to anyone who wanted to express an opposing view.

You can see that it is important to have a clear understanding of current events and of the status quo; otherwise, you might find yourself "tilting at windmills." If you did not know that the fairness doctrine had been dropped by the FCC as a requirement for broadcasters, you might find yourself arguing for the adoption of a policy that had already been accepted.

The status quo is an important consideration when you are deciding whether to support or oppose a proposition that is on an election ballot. Sometimes the wording of a proposition is misleading, and if you are not careful, you may wind up voting in favor of something that you actually oppose. Remember this: Anytime you vote "yes" on a proposition, you are voting for a change in the status quo; when you vote "no," you are voting to retain the status quo. So it is necessary that you know what the status quo is. For example, the proposition may pertain to the construction of a new dam, and you may want to prevent it from being built. The status quo may be that permission to build the dam has been granted, and the proposition would be to rescind the permission. So you would vote "yes" on the proposition because you are *opposed* to the dam.

Once you have established in your own mind what side of the issue you want to be on, you can begin to consider what information you need to include in your presentation that will have an effect on the way the people in your audience draw their conclusions.

COGNITIVE DISSONANCE

When people establish for themselves a belief structure pertaining to issues they regard as important, they like to hear facts that support what they believe to be true. They also want to believe that they are acting in accordance with what they are convinced is the truth. For example, if they are making contributions to a television evangelist, they want to believe that their money is going for a good cause. To make sure that consistency prevails in their lives, they likely will associate with other people who have similar beliefs and tune in to media presentations that say what they want to hear. When they are confronted with information that conflicts with their beliefs, they will probably try to find a way to reject it or refute it. To illustrate the point, consider the case of evangelist Jim Bakker: When he was accused of having an illicit love affair and charged with misusing funds that were contributed to his PTL foundation, his supporters had a difficult time reconciling the new information with what they wanted to believe was true. Some of them attempted to discredit the sources of the critical information, claiming that the charges were false; others tried to minimize the importance of the accusations, maintaining that Jim Bakker was doing such good work that a few minor infractions and indulgences should not be cause for criticism or prosecution. Still others experienced a great deal of discomfort, faced with the realization that what they had believed to be true apparently was not.

The painful experience of being confronted with irrefutable evidence that conflicts with a deep-seated belief structure is what sociologists call *cognitive dissonance.*[4] It is sometimes referred to as "buyer's remorse" because it is similar to the feeling you have when you are dissatisfied with a purchase you have made. The feeling is especially strong when it was an expensive item and was something you thought you wanted for a long time. The TV viewers who bought into Jim Bakker's evangelistic movement did not give up easily when the truth came out; in fact, many of them continued to support the foundation even after they knew what he had done with the money. What this says is that when people don't really want

[4] L. Festinger, *A Theory of Cognitive Dissonance,* Stanford University Press, Stanford, Calif., 1957.

to change, they can always find a reason for not doing it. The condition of cognitive dissonance does not necessarily bring about the alteration of a belief or commitment, but it frequently is the step that precedes such a change. This is why we say that cognitive dissonance is the first stage of persuasion.

What you need to recognize when you are delivering a speech to convince is that some people in the audience may have an intense commitment to the point of view that you are about to attack. You are not going to be successful if you make unsupported accusations. To claim simply that a charitable institution has been irresponsible with its money is not going to have any effect on those who fervently believe in what it is doing. You will have to provide documented evidence that significantly challenges the credibility of the institution. The information must be damaging enough so that opponents are required to refute the charges in order to logically maintain the belief which they previously held. Even when you are able to produce this kind of evidence, the people you are trying to persuade may still not be convinced. If, however, you create in them the condition of cognitive dissonance, you can consider your efforts to be successful. Persuasion generally does not occur immediately after a single speech, so be patient.

PERSUASIVE INFORMATION

In its raw state, information is rhetorically neutral. It can be employed to develop any kind of a speech, whether the purpose is to inform, to convince, to entertain, or to motivate. The significance of the material you gather is not always self-evident—it can enlighten, persuade, amuse, or inspire, depending on the way it is used.

Information that is intended to be persuasive must be presented in a persuasive framework. The listener must be able to perceive two things: that the new evidence is valid and that it conflicts with previous beliefs. It is up to the speaker to facilitate both these conditions in order for the first step of persuasion to take place. The perceived validity of the information will depend on the confidence the listener has in the speaker as well as in the source of the speaker's information. The extent to which the information conflicts with previous beliefs depends on the way the speaker integrates the information into his or her claim.

The information used to support a speech to convince is called *evidence*. Evidence could, of course, be physical as well as rhetorical, but right now we are primarily concerned with the latter. Rhetorical evidence can be in the form of statistics, testimony, specific instances, case histories, or any of the other forms mentioned earlier. When your purpose is to lead the audience to a conclusion you want them to accept, your evidence must be presented in a way that will accomplish that end. Extraneous information should be deleted from the speech, and contrary material should be justified in some way. What do you do when you come across evidence in your research that seems to contradict your thesis? You could leave it out, of course, but then someone might ask you about it during the question period. A better plan would be to include it in the speech, but refute it. If you can't refute it, explain to your audience how you are still able to take the position you do in light of what seems to be conflicting evidence.

Part of the strategy of developing a speech to convince is to phrase your information in a way that supports your claim. It's important to remember that facts do not speak for themselves; the interpretation you give to the facts is what will influence the audience. For example, you might be giving a speech in support of government-funded health insurance. While researching the topic you discover that 87 percent of the people in the United States are already covered by some sort of medical plan. If you simply present the evidence and let it stand without comment, you are suggesting that there is not much reason for your proposal. But you don't have to phrase it that way. You can say that 13 percent of Americans—33 million people—have no coverage at all. That information communicates a much different message.

CONSTRUCTING AN ARGUMENTATIVE CASE

The speaker who addresses an audience that is listening critically must know how to construct an effective argumentative case. To persuade an audience through reason rather than through emotion requires that we have an understanding of the theory behind argumentation. An argument is more than just a statement of fact or the expression of an opinion. It is a combination of parts, each with a specific function, and all of them have to work together. Let's begin our analysis of the theory by defining some of the commonly used terminology.

Advancing a Claim

A *claim* is a sentence or phrase that expresses a belief which you have arrived at through reason. By itself it does not pose as a statement of fact, but it does imply that there is factual evidence which supports it. It could also be called an *assertion* or a *contention;* in your outline it might be one of the main headings. For example, a claim would be as follows: "Cigarette smoke is harmful to the health of people who breathe it." Note that a claim is different from an opinion. You can express an opinion anytime you want whether you have evidence or not. When you say, "I don't like cigarette smoking," you are not constructing an argument, you are simply stating your opinion. It's your right to do that whether you have evidence or not. But when you advance a claim, you are required to provide factual support.

Using Evidence to Support a Claim

Evidence is the factual support behind the claim, and it must be linked to the claim before we can say that an argument has been advanced. In other words, evidence does not speak for itself. The reason it does not is that it can often be interpreted in a number of different ways. It is your job as a speaker to provide that interpretation in order for the audience to know what you mean. Here is an example of a piece of evidence: "Cigarette smoke contains carbon monoxide." If the statement were allowed to stand by itself, we would not know what significance the speaker might be attaching to it. The evidence needs to be linked to the claim in order to form an argument:

> Cigarette smoke is harmful to the health of people who breathe it because it contains carbon monoxide.

Providing a Warrant to Reinforce the Evidence

In order for an argument to be firmly established, the significance of the evidence may need to be reinforced. In other words the audience might be saying to themselves, "Why is that evidence so important?" Remember, we observed in an earlier chapter that listeners may not be able to see how a piece of information is linked to the idea that you want them to accept. So, it might be necessary to explain how the evidence contributes to the support of the claim. In the theory of argumentation, a linking statement of this kind is called a *warrant*. To establish that the evidence in the smoking argument is really important, the speaker might add, "Carbon monoxide is a deadly poison."

Forming a Thesis

When you develop a series of arguments, they will begin to form a pattern and you can start thinking about phrasing your thesis. In an earlier chapter we said that the thesis is the purpose or main idea of the speech that you want your audience to accept. When you are dealing with a controversial topic, you have to recognize that your thesis will probably meet opposition. It needs to be expressed in such a way that it addresses all the claims you make in the speech and accounts for all the evidence. On the subject of smoking your thesis might look like this:

If smoking is to remain legal in the United States, we need to do everything we can to warn people of the dangers, prevent the younger generation from starting to smoke, help smokers to quit, and protect the health of nonsmokers who are forced to live and work with those who smoke.

Qualifying the Thesis

There is one final element you might need to add in order for your argumentation to be complete. You may find it necessary to take exceptions into consideration and deal with them by making a *qualifying statement*. In the example used above, the qualifying statement is "If smoking is to remain legal." What you are doing here is saying to your audience that you are not suggesting that smoking be outlawed. The qualifier gives credibility to your thesis so that listeners know that you are taking a reasoned and responsible point of view.

When you combine the claim, the evidence, the warrant, the thesis, and the qualifier, you have a strong argumentative *case*. Here is the way it would look in outline form:

Avoiding the Hazards of Smoking

Attention Statement: Everything we know about cigarette smoking tells us that it is harmful to health and has no socially redeeming qualities.

Thesis Statement: If smoking is to remain legal in the United States, we need to do everything we can to warn people of the dangers, prevent the younger generation from starting to smoke, help smokers to quit, and protect the health of those who are forced to live and work with people who smoke.

I Smoke from cigarettes is harmful to everyone who breathes it.
  A It is life-threatening to the smoker.
    1 Contains carbon monoxide, tars, and nicotine.
    2 Lung and heart diseases account for 350,000 deaths per year.
  B It is harmful to other people who breathe the smoke.
    1 Effects of secondary smoke.
    2 Effects on people with lung problems.
II Every day new smokers are taking up the habit.
  A More people are starting than are quitting.
    1 51 million smokers in U.S.
    2 Tobacco industry targets specific groups.
    3 Most new smokers are young people.

B Smoking is addictive.
   1 Report by former surgeon general, C. Everett Koop.
   2 85% of smokers want to quit but can't.
   3 75% relapse rate; harder to break than the drug habit.
III Education is not enough; we need to enact controls.
  A Warning labels that smoking is addictive.
  B Ban on cigarette machines.
  C Remove government subsidies of tobacco industry.
  D Restrict smoking in public places.

Conclusion: We certainly must have compassion for smokers; they are victims, not offenders. But their habit is placing themselves and others at risk, which makes smoking a social problem as well as an individual problem.

EMOTIONAL APPEALS

The best approach for developing a speech to convince is to present strong supporting evidence whenever it's available, but there are occasions when it may be more effective to base your appeals on values you hold that you know are shared by members of the audience. Attorney Clarence Darrow said that when the defense of a person on trial is a matter of justice, you do not have to give the jury reasons to acquit the client; you make them want to vote for acquittal and they'll find their own reasons.

Shared Values

There are times when our convictions are founded upon emotional feelings rather than fact, and the message that we want our audience to accept is not one which can be supported by evidence and clinical studies. For example, we all share a belief in justice and the protection of human rights, and we don't require that documented proof of their value be provided. People in the audience are going to be moved by a speaker whose appeal is founded on the same principles to which they, themselves, subscribe, and who conveys a sincere and dedicated commitment to the moral tenets basic to their belief structure.

There may be times when rhetorical evidence does not tell the whole story and may actually be counterproductive to achieving the purpose of the speech. Facts alone do not have the inspirational quality that move people to take courage when hard times and even disaster are facing them. During the depression years of the 1930s the social conditions in this country looked extremely bleak. If Franklin Roosevelt had done nothing but relate statistics to describe the economic circumstances, people might have fallen into a state of despair. Instead, he was able to reach them at the emotional level by speaking to them on a regular basis in the comfortable setting that came to be known as a "fireside chat." Instead of stock market quotations, he gave them words of encouragement and told them, "the only thing you have to fear is fear itself." To a large extent it was the personal integrity and sense of confidence that President Roosevelt projected which gave people hope and eventually led the country out of the depression.

In order to be successful in making emotional appeals work for you it is necessary that you identify the values you share with the audience and project them with a sense of conviction. Probably the most important quality you need is sincerity. If you attempt to apply lofty values to trivial issues, the phoniness will become immediately apparent to your listeners. To make the claim that you are fighting for freedom against totalitarian aggressors who are raising the parking meter fees will not inspire confidence in your sincerity.

Differences in Applying Values

Shared values are much easier to establish at a high level of abstraction. For example, we might all be able to agree with the generalization that the lives of innocent people should be protected. It's when we begin to apply those values to specific cases and define what we mean by *innocent lives* that we find ourselves confronted by differing opinions. Those who oppose the legal status of abortion would include an unborn fetus in the definition of "innocent lives." People who support a woman's right to have an abortion would argue that life does not begin until after birth. This issue is a particularly difficult one because the underlying principle that forms the basis of what people believe is not a matter that can be established with factual evidence.

YOUR PERSONAL INTEGRITY

The use of emotional appeals in a speech is, in itself, a controversial issue. There are some critics who would contend that decisions ought to be based on reason alone and that an attempt to arouse emotional feelings is an unscrupulous rhetorical device. That may be true if the speaker is feigning emotions as a means of manipulating an audience into accepting a claim that would not stand up to the test of reason. But there are approaches you might find useful to consider that are generally regarded as being within the parameters of ethical behavior.

The Depth of Your Feelings

If the feelings you have about an issue are genuinely strong, you are not deceiving an audience by expressing them. In fact, if you fail to communicate sincere concern for the plight of people who deserve compassion, the audience might regard you as cold and uncaring. The speaker who wants to engage the emotions of the audience must begin with his or her own emotional involvement. Listeners tend to respond to the mood that is set by the speaker.[5] You can't expect the audience to be moved unless you are willing to speak from the heart and convey the depth of your own feelings.

Your Own Experience

Selecting a topic in which you have had personal experience is an excellent way to help establish for yourself the credibility that you want the audience to perceive. If you are able to say "I know because I was there," your listeners are more likely to pay attention than they would if you were making a secondhand report. There are a few caveats, however, to this approach. First of all, you don't want to come across as a braggart. If the audience gets the idea that you are telling about your experiences in order to extol your own virtues, they may reject your claim regardless of the merit it may have. Secondly, make sure you are able to keep your emotions from getting out of control. If your topic is child abuse, for example, and you yourself were an abused child, you may be able to make your point in a very powerful way. But if you can't talk about the subject without breaking down, you might find that the public speaking mode of communication makes the experience too painful for you to handle.

Language of Emotion

The reason for employing emotional appeals in a speech is to cause people to pay attention and be moved to think or act upon what you have said. In order to accomplish that, you have to use language that will create an impact and construct your phrases and sentences so that they will be remembered. The kind of inspirational language that we hear in speeches with lofty purposes often is of a rather general nature, and we are seldom able to trace a specific action to any one particular message. We do know, however, that some phrases are remembered and are often quoted; we also believe that behavior can be profoundly affected by words that touch people at the emotional level. In his inaugural address, John F. Kennedy might

---

[5] James R. Andrews, *Public Speaking: Principles into Practice,* Macmillan, New York, 1987, p. 138.

"The glow from that fire can truly light the world."

have made a simple request for people to volunteer for government service. Instead, he reached out in a much more dramatic way:

> The energy, the faith, the devotion which we bring to this endeavor will light our country and all who serve it—and the glow from that fire can truly light the world. And so, my fellow Americans, ask not what your country can do for you; ask what you can do for your country.

The thought, phrasing, and quality of the language makes this a great speech, but even more important is that people *acted* on the words. Kennedy's challenge resulted in the formation of the Peace Corps, and thousands of young people from all over the nation answered the call to serve their country in the cause of peace.

THE CREDIBILITY OF THE SPEAKER

Having gone to all the trouble of gathering the information, organizing it, and practicing the delivery, can you be sure that the audience is going to believe what you say? If you are known in the community and have acquired a reputation for being honest and well informed, your words will carry considerable weight. But what if people are hearing you for the first time? How will they know if your information is accurate and if you are telling the truth? The capacity to establish your credibility when you are unknown to the audience is one of the most important variables in determining success in public speaking.

If people are going to trust that you know what you are talking about, you have to speak as though you do. Make sure you are familiar with your own evidence. If you appear to be seeing it for the first time on your note cards, your credibility is going to take a nosedive. Cite your sources whenever you need to so that your audience knows that you are not making things up out of your own head. And above all, make sure that you let them know that what you are saying is what you believe.

One of the most difficult judicial decisions made in recent times by the United States Senate was the confirmation of Judge Clarence Thomas for Supreme Court Justice when charges of sexual harassment were brought against him by Professor Anita Hill. The Senate Judiciary Committee made every effort it could to find factual evidence on which they could base their decision, but ultimately it was a question of one person's word against another. Someone was not telling the truth, but both parties were reputable, professional people who appeared to be equally credible. The choice was made by the Senate in favor of Judge Thomas, but by the very slim margin of 52 to 48.

Don't make the mistake of assuming that your sincerity will be self-evident. Even though there are people who say they can tell whether or not someone is telling the truth, the evidence indicates the contrary. Those who claim they can perceive the sincerity of a speaker are just guessing and are wrong half the time. What people in the audience do is observe and evaluate characteristics of delivery—the posture, the gestures, the facial expressions, the eye contact, and the vocal inflection—all the features that appear to be the indicators of integrity. But we know that the effective application of these speaking techniques is available to anyone, whether they are honest or not. This tells us that just *being* sincere isn't enough; you have to know how to *project* sincerity if you want people to believe what you say. Whether you like the notion or not, the audience is going to apply subjective criteria in making their determination of whether or not they are going to believe you. Truth is not self-evident. The only way it can prevail is if it is advocated by honest and just men and women who are effective in their communication. Sixteen hundred years ago St. Augustine wrote:

> Who would dare to say that truth should stand in the person of its defenders, unarmed against lying, so that they who wish to urge falsehoods may know how to make their listeners benevolent, or attentive, or docile in their presentation, while the defenders of truth are ignorant of that art? Should they speak briefly, clearly, and plausibly while the defenders of truth speak so that they tire their listeners, make themselves difficult to understand and what they have to say dubious? . . . Who is so foolish as to think this to be wisdom?[6]

[6] Saint Augustine, *On Christian Doctrine,* Book Four, II, D. W. Robertson, Jr. (trans.). Copyright © 1958 by Macmillan Publishing Company. Reprinted by permission of the publisher.

EXERCISE

Develop a speech on gun control using the information cited below. Remember that evidence does not speak for itself, so you will have to select the data you want to use and combine each fact with a claim that supports your point of view. The thesis you establish and the recommendation you make can be of your own invention. You do not need to use all the information in your speech, but you should be able to respond to questions that members of the audience might ask. The statements below are listed at random; arrange them in a logical sequence and combine them in outline form with your thesis, main headings, and conclusion.

• Twenty-two people were killed in Killeen, Texas, on October 16, 1991, by a berserk gunman firing a 9 mm pistol, which holds a clip of seventeen rounds.

• Firearms are involved in more than 30,000 deaths each year in the United States.

• There are 70 million gun owners in the United States.

• In January 1989 Patrick Purdy killed five schoolchildren on a playground in Stockton, California, with an AK-47 assault rifle.

• Violent crimes continued to rise in New York and Washington after passage of strict firearm control measures.

• 87 percent of the U.S. population say they would support a federal law to require a seven-day waiting period and background check for the purchase of a handgun.

• The National Rifle Association has certified 26,000 instructors and trains 750,000 students each year in the use of firearms.

• The Supreme Court has upheld the right of Morton Grove, Illinois, to ban firearms in the city limits.

• 3 percent of the members of the National Rifle Association are women.

• Colt Industries withdrew one of its semiautomatic rifles from the market after the shooting massacre in Stockton, California.

• The Second Amendment to the Constitution says, "A well regulated Militia, being necessary to the security of a free State, the right of the people to keep and bear Arms shall not be infringed."

QUESTIONS FOR REVIEW

1 How do you define *coercion, manipulation, bribery,* and *deception?* In what way do they all differ from persuasion? Why do we say that free choice is an important element of persuasion?

2 What did Aristotle mean by the *modes of proof*—the logos, the pathos, and the ethos?

3 How did it happen that Norma McCorvey became a speaker rather than just a house painter? What role did she play in the 1973 decision of *Roe v. Wade?*

4 What is meant by the term *status quo?* Which way do you vote on a ballot measure when you favor the status quo? Explain.

5 What is meant by the term *cognitive dissonance?* What do people tend to do in order to avoid experiencing cognitive dissonance?

6 Why do we say that information in its raw form is not persuasive? What do you have to add to the information to make it persuasive?

7 In the theory of argumentation what is meant by a *claim?* What is meant by *evidence,* and how does evidence affect the claim?

8 What is the difference between physical and rhetorical evidence?

9 What is a *warrant* for a claim? Why is a warrant sometimes necessary in order for an argumentative statement to be clear?

10 What is a *thesis statement?* What role does it play in a speech to convince?

11 What is the most important personal quality needed to make the emotional appeals of a speaker effective? Why is it not a good idea to apply lofty values to trivial issues?

12 What are three approaches a speaker might use as a means of appealing to the emotions of an audience?

13 What is meant by the *credibility* of the speaker?

14 What did St. Augustine have to say about the defenders of truth in relation to learning effective methods of persuasion?

PART **THREE**

THE SPEAKER

CHAPTER 7

THE SPEAKER'S FRAME OF MIND

If you can honestly say that you do not suffer from speech anxiety, you can skip this chapter. I certainly don't want to call your attention to something that is not a problem for you in the first place. But if you do feel the proverbial butterflies in the stomach, you can be assured that you have a great deal of company, and there are steps you can take to relieve the condition. It is quite understandable that you may have anxieties about giving a speech, and there is nothing unusual about wanting to shy away from it. Public speaking generally ranks close to the top of the list of experiences that people say they fear the most. The fact that you do have anxieties simply means that you regard the situation as important enough to warrant concern. If that concern makes you put more effort into your preparation, speech fright can actually work in your favor. I have heard some excellent speeches given by people who were highly stressed but well prepared, and very poor ones given by those who were completely relaxed but had nothing to say. My conclusion is that anxiety itself need not be an inhibiting factor; however, if the fear disrupts your thought process while you are speaking, make an effort to set up a plan for yourself to prevent that from happening. Taking a speech course will help, but there are also other things you can do.

THOROUGH PREPARATION

Sometimes I hear a student in my class say, "Let me give my speech first so I can get it over with." If you have ever had this feeling, it probably means that you are not motivated to give the speech because you want the message to be heard; you are viewing the experience only as something to be endured. If you really want to overcome speech fright, direct your attention to the importance of what it is that you are going to say.

Almost all the literature pertaining to stress reduction in oral communication emphasizes that making thorough preparation is the best way to deal with public speaking anxiety. In the years I have been teaching speech I have found that it is often the least prepared students who have the most anxiety. It seems that anxiety often begins not at the moment speakers step onto the podium, but at the very beginning stage when they are planning what they are going to say. Think about that and see if it applies to you. You might be going through the motions of preparation when you really don't want to give the speech at all. Sometimes students will begin the speech, but their volume is so low they can't be heard. What's happening is that subconsciously they don't really *want* to be heard. The reason for this may be that they lack confidence in the quality of the message and fear that it may not be adequate. Speech anxiety is often used as an excuse by people who really mean that they are not prepared. There is a certain logic to that thinking: If you don't prepare a speech, you can't be expected to give one. And if you are required to speak anyway and it goes badly, you can say, "You see, I told you I couldn't give a speech." That rationale is called "creative avoidance." It may get you out of having to give speeches, but it doesn't help you cope with the problem, and it tends to reinforce the anxieties. A better procedure is to confront the fears and deal with them.

Most of the evidence we have pertaining to techniques for overcoming speech anxiety is anecdotal. Some people have reported success by taking a walk just before speaking or doing breathing exercises. These methods can't hurt and you should try anything that works, but if you begin to feel anxiety even as you are preparing the speech, it is important that you take remedial measures early. Experts who teach public speaking in the business world list preparation, positive thinking, visualization, relaxation, and confidence in yourself as the key elements in reducing anxiety.[1] But the process begins with forming a positive attitude.

FORMING ATTITUDES

A great deal of your anxiety is related to the attitude you have toward public speaking. The word *attitude* simply means "the way you lean." If you have a positive attitude, you lean *toward* something; if you have a negative attitude, you lean *away* from it. Attitudes develop over a long period

[1] Robert Edward Burns, "Combating Speech Anxiety," *Public Relations Journal*, March 1991, p. 28.

of time, and we never know when they start. Your attitude toward public speaking may have begun when you were very young and your parents had you stand up to recite a poem for company. Later on, you probably had to do "show and tell" in school, and your attitude was reinforced. If those were good experiences for you, the attitude you have toward public speaking may be positive; if they were bad experiences, you probably have a negative attitude. The point is that you did not *choose* the attitude intentionally; it just happened.

Attitudes are formed out of your experiences, not the way they really happened but the way you *perceived* they happened. If someone laughed when you were doing "show and tell," you may have thought the laughter was directed at you, and you became embarrassed by it. The laughter may actually have been totally unrelated to anything you did, but if you thought at the time the other students were laughing at you, that's the way the experience was recorded in your subconscious mind. What's more, every time you recall the experience, the memory of it is reinforced until it becomes a permanent part of your mental data bank.

It's that kind of data that makes us feel the way we do. In later life when we are confronted by new situations, such as an opportunity to give a speech, we automatically search the memory banks in our subconscious mind to recall occasions that might be similar. If the previous experiences were unpleasant ones, we might be inclined to say "No, thank you" and make up some excuse for not doing it without ever giving our conscious mind a chance to review the decision.

BUILDING SELF-ESTEEM

The attitudes we hold constitute a significant part of our self-concept—the image we have in our minds as to who we are and what is or is not appropriate behavior for us. Self-esteem is how we feel about that image.[2] A positive self-concept means we have high self-esteem. If we feel confident that we are able to deal with a wide variety of challenges that life hands to us, we will be willing to take risks and explore opportunities that lead us into new experiences. If our self-esteem is low, we might be reluctant to do anything that would jeopardize our security or expose us to criticism.

Messages to Ourselves

Our self-concept is reinforced by the messages we give ourselves in the form of thoughts or even words spoken out loud. Have you ever heard

[2] Em Griffin, *A First Look at Communication Theory*, McGraw-Hill, New York, 1991, p. 70.

We all have an image of ourself, but how did the image get there?

yourself saying, "Boy, am I dumb!" Listen sometime to what is being said by students when they come into the classroom on the day they are to give their speech. You will hear a great deal of disparaging language that can result only in creating a negative self-concept. Students will say "I wish I didn't have to do this" and "I'm not ready" or "My topic is going to be really boring." This is called *self-talk*, and it has a profound effect on the way we think about ourselves. The negative self-talk affects our attitudes, and our attitudes in turn affect our self-talk. The result is a downward spiral of our self-esteem that often leads to poor performance. What we do is talk ourselves into falling below our true potential, not because of low ability but because of the image we create of ourselves. The unfortunate thing is that it all happens without our even being aware of it.

But the spiral effect can work the other way, too. Positive messages can lead to successful performance, successful performance leads to high self-esteem, and high self-esteem means we give ourselves more positive messages. It all gets back to that self-concept, or self-image. How do we change the picture of ourselves from something we don't like and don't want to an image that more accurately portrays what we can do and really want to do?

COGNITIVE RESTRUCTURING

If you find that any part of your self-image is not serving you well, you can change it. We call the process *cognitive restructuring*—that means you can redesign the way you think about yourself so that your self-image becomes more like what you *want* it to be. This process is more than just a pill to calm your nerves; it is a "refined, systematic technique that alters the cognitive dimension of anxiety."[3] The idea is not a new one, nor does it always go by the same name. Maxwell Maltz calls it "psycho-cybernetics," and he describes it in the following way:

> Whether we realize it or not, each of us carries about with us a mental blueprint or picture of ourselves. It may be vague and ill-defined to our conscious gaze. In fact, it may not be consciously recognizable at all. But it is there, complete down to the last detail. This self-image is our own conception of the "sort of person I am." It has been built up from our own beliefs about ourselves. But most of these beliefs have unconsciously been formed from our past experiences, our successes and failures, our humiliations, our triumphs, and the way other people have reacted to us, especially in early childhood. From all these we mentally construct a "self" (or a picture of a self). Once an idea or a belief about ourselves goes into this picture it becomes "true" as far as we personally are concerned. We do not question its validity, but proceed to act upon it just as if it were true.[4]

[3] William J. Fremouw and Michael D. Scott, "Cognitive Restructuring: An Alternative Method for the Treatment of Communication Apprehension," *Communication Education*, May 1979, p. 130.
[4] Maxwell Maltz, *Psycho-Cybernetics*, copyright © 1974 by Dr. Maxwell Maltz. Reprinted by permission of Pocket Books, a division of Simon & Schuster, Inc.

Regulating Your Self-Image

You may have all the potential in the world to give excellent speeches, but if you have somehow acquired the notion that you stumble over words and forget what you want to say when you are in front of an audience, that's probably what will happen. Your psycho-cybernetic mechanism will go to work to see that the image you have of yourself becomes reality.

The term *cybernetic* refers to a self-regulating mechanism, like a thermostat. A thermostat will allow the temperature to rise and fall within a limited margin, but if the room gets too hot or too cold, it cuts in and makes an adjustment. You have a similar kind of mechanism in your mind that tends to confine your behavior to what your self-image has said is appropriate for you. If you begin to deviate too much from that central zone, you start to feel uncomfortable and you adjust your behavior to bring yourself more in line with your picture. The interesting thing about the mechanism is that it will regulate your behavior whether you're doing better or worse than you think you should be. You may have observed this phenomenon if you play sports—let's say tennis. Maybe you are playing someone who always beats you, but in this set you are ahead 5 to 4; you are serving, and the score is 30 to 15. Suddenly you start thinking, "I'm playing a better game than I have ever played before!" What happens? Your psycho-cybernetic mechanism goes to work and tells you to get back where you belong. So you start blowing shots, you lose the next three games, and she beats you 7 to 5.

Why does this not happen to champions? Because they have adjusted their psycho-cybernetic mechanisms to the high end of the scale where they have to win in order to feel comfortable. That seems like a good way to become a winner, and it is. However, be sure to heed a word of warning: When you do that, you place yourself under a great deal of stress, and the discomfort of losing can be quite severe.

Comfort Zones

What our self-image does is to establish for us behavior patterns that make us feel comfortable. If we find ourselves forced to do something that is in conflict with our self-image, we become stressed and start resisting in any way we can. Attending a lecture may be well within your comfort zone, but *giving* a lecture perhaps is not. People who have rich, fulfilling lives are those who have a broad comfort zone—one that permits them to feel OK about themselves in a variety of situations. If you perceive that your comfort zone is narrow and want to expand it, how do you go about doing it? That's what cognitive restructuring is all about.

Sometimes people try to make changes in their behavior patterns by writing resolutions for themselves; often this is a ritual that takes place on New Year's Day. But generally people who sit down on January 1 and list all the things they intend to do in the coming year wind up forgetting what they wrote even before the ink is dry. Often they include on their list what they believe they *ought* to do rather than what they really *want* to do. What's more, change in their behavior fails to come about because the picture they have of themselves is still the same as it was before. When you try to do something that is in conflict with your self-image, you make yourself very uncomfortable. So in order to bring about change in your behavior you have to change your picture. The question is which one should you change first? If you have a strong resolve, you might try changing the behavior first—just grit your teeth and do it regardless of how uncomfortable it makes you feel. Eventually, if you have successful experiences, your self-image might also change. But if the stress level is very high and you get no satisfaction out of what you are doing, you will ultimately abandon that behavior. That's why it is important for you to give yourself affirmation for what you are doing, because it is the verbal messages that you give yourself that will change your self-image.

Adjusting Your Psycho-Cybernetic Mechanism

The key to all of this is your psycho-cybernetic mechanism—you need to know how to set it to a challenging, but realistic, point. If you decide you want to embark upon this program, what you will be doing is restructuring the way you picture your communication behavior and your attitude toward being a public speaker. But this time, instead of letting it all happen at random, you will be selecting intentionally the skill level that you want. To begin the process, you must decide that you really have the desire to be a person who is able and willing to speak to groups. The choice must be made freely without pressure from your parents, teachers, or anyone else. This process is not going to work if you are merely trying to comply with goals that someone else has set for you. If you can honestly say that you want to make some changes, you are ready for the next phase of the process. Take out a notebook and start making the following entries:

1 Goals First, decide specifically what you want to be able to do. You don't have to set a goal of having the ability to address large audiences on lofty topics. You may want to begin by saying you would like to be able to talk to small groups of fifteen or twenty people on subjects pertaining to your business or hobby; you may simply want to be able to speak up during class discussion. Whatever your goal is, get a picture of it in your mind as you write it down.

2 Limitations Identify any real limitations that you will have to deal with in order to attain your goal. For example, if you are a recent immigrant from another country, you may be struggling with English as a second language; you may have a speech impediment or a learning disability. These are real obstacles that will not go away just by reconstructing your self-image. You may have to enter into a specialized program to bring about the change you want. What psycho-cybernetics can do, however, is to make it possible for you to confront those obstacles and not allow them to defeat you.

3 Assets Your next entry will be a list of characteristics and abilities you have that will assist you in achieving your goals. You may say, for example, that you really enjoy relating to people, that you listen well and remember what you hear, that you read a lot and have a good vocabulary, or that you are interested in a variety of topics or have some expertise in a particular subject. Put down on your list anything you think will contribute to your ability to give a good speech.

4 Previous Experiences Even if you have never made a speech before, there are occasions in the past when you have communicated effectively to someone. Think back and recall times when you have been able to say something just the way you wanted to say it. It may have been in conversation with a small group of friends or in a class discussion; perhaps it was at a meeting or on a radio talk show. Try to remember what the subject was and what point you were making. Recreate the episode in your mind, and as you write it down, reinforce the good feeling you had about speaking on that occasion.

5 Topics for Speeches Make a list of topics that you would be able to address after you have had some time for preparation. You could list things you know about already, or you could include subjects you would be interested in researching. What this list will do is help you relieve the anxiety of feeling that you don't have anything to talk about. It will also help you focus on the subject matter of the speech rather than on your nervousness in delivering it.

6 Affirmations Select five or six items from your list of assets and previous experiences, and write them on a separate piece of paper in the form of affirmations. An *affirmation* is a positive and realistic statement you can honestly make about yourself that will reinforce the best characteristics you have at the present time. The statement should be phrased in such a way as to replace your negative self-talk with assertions that are designed to improve your self-concept and raise your self-esteem. They need to be

An affirmation is a postive statement you can make about yourself.

fairly specific so you can get a clear picture of what you do or have done that substantiates the messages you are giving to yourself. For example, a list of affirmations might look like this:

- I am well-acquainted with environmental problems and have an appreciation for wilderness areas. I have given thought to conservation measures, and I can elaborate on my opinions with sound and concrete evidence.
- I have good conviction in my voice, and people take me seriously when I speak. In social conversations my ideas are heard and respected.
- The nervousness I sometimes feel when I am speaking to groups does not inhibit my ability to say what I want to say.

These are merely examples of affirmations. The ones you write for yourself must be your own. Be sure you don't exaggerate or make false claims. You have to believe with all sincerity that what you are saying is realistic and that you want these qualities to be the prominent features of your personality. It is important that you phrase them in the first person, present tense ("I am . . ." not "I will be . . .") because the idea is to reinforce the positive characteristics you have now, not the vague speculation of what you think you could be in the future. People who continually say to themselves, "Someday I will become . . ." usually put off indefinitely making any constructive changes.

IMPRINTING THE NEW IMAGE

Once you have written your list of affirmations in this form, carry the paper around with you and read the statements to yourself several times a day for about two weeks. Soon you will find that when you change your self-talk, the image you have of yourself will also begin to change. And as your image changes, so will your feelings and your behavior.

Richard Weaver, professor of speech communication at Bowling Green State University, defines imaging as the process of creating mental pictures that substitute for the real thing.[5] In a speech delivered to the Golden Key National Honor Society at Ann Arbor, Michigan, he described how he got through college by creating in his mind an image of himself as a university student. You must understand, however, that it is not the image alone that does the trick. What makes this method work is your accepting responsibility for behaving in a way that is commensurate with the image you have created. Just picturing yourself as a student is not enough. You must be able to see yourself doing what a student does—going to class, spending time in the library, staying up late at night studying for an exam. If those pictures do not appeal to you, a little voice inside your head is going to say, "Who do you think you're kidding?"

If you can really convince yourself that you are a person who fits the image of a public speaker, there are a number of ways to imprint your new self-concept. Take some time when you are alone to relax in a comfortable chair and create an image in your mind of yourself going through the process of preparing and delivering a speech. Picture yourself writing the outline and thinking about what you are going to say. Then get a picture of yourself as you come into the room on the day you are going to give your speech. Get the feeling of waiting until you are introduced, then going to the front of the room, stepping up to the podium, and turning to face your audience. As you create all these mental images, keep thinking to yourself that you are well prepared, you have sound ideas, and your supporting evidence is interesting as well as factual. Now picture yourself as you deliver

---

[5] Richard L. Weaver II "Self-Fulfillment through Imaging," from the keynote address delivered at the induction ceremony, Golden Key National Honor Society, Ann Arbor, Mich., Nov. 8, 1990; *Vital Speeches*, Jan. 15, 1991, p. 217.

the speech. Try to get a clear image of what you are doing and how the audience is responding. See yourself making good eye contact, gesturing, and maintaining a relaxed and composed posture. Imagine as much detail as you can—the way you are dressed, the pacing of your speech, the energy you are projecting, and the reaction of the audience. In other words, picture it just the way you want it to be.

The value of this exercise is that you desensitize yourself to the real experience. When the time comes actually to give the speech, you will already have been through it and will know what it is like.

REWARDS OF SPEAKING

To become an effective speaker, it is essential to develop and maintain a positive attitude toward what you are doing. If you simply endure the experience with reluctance and distaste, you will not have a good feeling before, during, or after the presentation. Consequently, the next time you do it, you will suffer the same anxiety, and it may be even worse. On the other hand, if you project to the audience that you like being there and believe that your message is important, they will respond in a positive way and reinforce your good feelings. Some of the rewards of speaking come in the form of applause and affirming statements that people make to you afterward. But you will find that the approval which makes the most difference is that which you give to yourself. Preparing and delivering public statements provides you with the opportunity to clarify your thoughts and values—and having the confidence of knowing that what you believe is clear in your mind contributes significantly to the upward spiral of your self-esteem. The method of cognitive restructuring makes it possible for you to communicate effectively with the most important person of all—yourself.

EXERCISE

Make arrangements to have one of your speeches videotaped; then watch the playback with your instructor or with someone who is able to give you constructive feedback. First, write down on a sheet of paper all the things you liked about the speech—the qualities of delivery, content, and organizational structure that you want your other speeches to contain. Next, make a list of the characteristics you can change and you would like to improve upon. (Don't worry if your voice sounds strange to you; you are probably just not used to hearing it on a recording device.) Keep the two lists and review them when you prepare your next speech. Mentally reinforce the qualities you like, and work on at least one item that you want to improve.

QUESTIONS FOR REVIEW

1 What is meant by the word *attitude*? How are attitudes formed, and how do they affect behavior?

2 How do you explain the fact that attitudes are generally not chosen intentionally?

3 What is meant by the term *self-concept*? How does self-talk affect self-concept?

4 What is meant by *self-esteem*? Why is a person with high self-esteem generally willing to take more risks?

5 What is meant by the *spiral effect*? What determines whether the self-esteem spiral goes up or down?

6 What is meant by the process of cognitive restructuring? How can it affect one's attitude toward public speaking?

7 What does Maxwell Maltz mean by the term *psycho-cybernetics*? What would be an example of a cybernetic mechanism?

8 How does psycho-cybernetics affect a player's performance in sports? What do champions do to make themselves winners? What is the disadvantage of doing what they do?

9 How does a narrow "comfort zone" reduce the richness of a person's life?

10 Why is it that New Year's resolutions are generally not successful in changing behavior?

11 What's wrong with having someone else set goals for you?

12 What advantage is there in recognizing your limitations as well as your assets while you are in the process of goal setting?

13 How might your previous experiences in communication situations affect your self-concept?

14 What is meant by an *affirmation*? Why should affirmations be written in the first person, present tense?

15 What are some ways to imprint affirmations? What is the value of imagining yourself going through the process of preparing and delivering a speech?

CHAPTER 8

DELIVERING THE MESSAGE

Henry Higgins, a character created by George Bernard Shaw and who appears in the play *My Fair Lady*, disparages the linguistic characteristics of the people in his own country when he says, "Why can't the English teach their children how to speak?" He is critical of the young woman, Liza Doolittle, who he claims will never be anything more than a miserable street peddler so long as she continues to corrupt the language with her cockney accent. Higgins says to his friend, "If you spoke as she does, sir, instead of the way you do, you might be selling flowers, too."

Almost everyone has an accent of one kind or another. Yours may be one that identifies you as a person who comes from a particular section of the country such as New England or the deep south, or it may be that English is your second language and you reveal your national origin when you speak. The accent itself does not need to be a problem as long as your diction is clear. But if you run words together, leave out syllables that need to be sounded, mispronounce words, and use careless grammar, your audience will be as critical of you as Henry Higgins was of Liza Doolittle.

THE USE OF LANGUAGE

I recommend to my students that they learn to speak standard English. While this may not be necessary on every occasion, some audiences will expect you to use proper grammar and correct syntax, and you will lose credibility if you are unable to do so. E. D. Hirsch makes the following observation in his book, *Cultural Literacy*:

> Linguists have used the term "standard written English" to describe both our written and spoken language, because they want to remind us that standard spoken English is based upon forms that have been fixed in dictionaries and grammars and are adhered to in books, magazines, and newspapers. Although standard written English has no intrinsic superiority to other languages and dialects, its stable written forms have now standardized the oral forms of the language spoken by educated Americans. The chief function of literacy is to make us masters of this standard instrument of knowledge and communication, thereby enabling us to give and receive complex information orally and in writing over time and space.[1]

You probably never think about the grammatical construction of your sentences when you speak. If you had good models in your early childhood years, you perhaps learned correct usage just by sound. Later, when you went to school, you were taught how to diagram a sentence and how to identify the nouns, verbs, adverbs, and adjectives. You learned that a sentence must have a subject and a predicate and must express a complete thought; that you use a semicolon or conjunction to connect two clauses, and place a period at the end of a sentence. You were also taught that the verb in the sentence must agree in person (I am, you are, he or she is) and in number (he doesn't, they don't) with its subject. You can probably recognize by sound that it is incorrect to say "I is" or "he don't." You may also remember that it is redundant, and therefore ungrammatical, to use double negatives when you are speaking English. (This is not the case in all languages.) People who say, "We didn't do nothing" reveal the fact that there are gaps in their education, and they should make an effort to learn the basic rules of grammar in order to communicate in a style that does not detract from their message.

Slang Expressions

What about the use of slang expressions? If they are used in moderation and are part of your own speaking style, they might keep a speech from sounding too "stuffy," but slang does tend to lower the intellectual tone of the speech. Sometimes a slang expression has more impact than the standard English equivalent. To say "I was blown away" has greater intensity than saying "I was very surprised." Given the right circumstances, the authentic use of slang can bring you closer to people who are comfortable with that kind of language and who appreciate your ability to speak it correctly. The danger is that a slang term used in the wrong way can make

---

[1] E. D. Hirsch, Jr., *Cultural Literacy*, Houghton Mifflin, Boston, 1987, p. 3.

you sound rather foolish. The primary criterion is that the expressions you use must be understandable to the audience. Slang is often spoken as a means of excluding outsiders, and that's not what you want to do when you are on the podium. Another problem with slang is that it tends to oversimplify complex concepts. To say that a particular event was "awesome" does not tell a great deal about the specific characteristics of what is being described. People who rely heavily on slang often neglect standard English terms that would be more precise, and frequently wind up saying such things as, "you know" and "you really had to be there."

Obscenity

In many social circles obscenity seems to be a common part of everyday conversation. Because it is, we may come to believe that it is equally acceptable in public address. We need to understand, however, that obscene words and references that are often tolerated in discussions with our friends, sound coarse and degrading when spoken from the podium. During the Senate confirmation hearings of Justice Clarence Thomas in October of 1991, we heard a great deal of graphic language and vulgar references, and we learned how unacceptable and repugnant such talk was to many listeners even when it was simply being quoted. Obscenity is not only crude but is generally sexist and racist, characteristics that make it even more offensive. People who rely heavily on the use of vulgarity identify themselves as being callous and insensitive, and consequently suffer a loss of credibility. Those who are offended by it may become distracted and fail to comprehend any legitimate point that the speaker might be making. Certainly there are some audiences who will find such remarks to be humorous and colorful, but seldom if ever does the use of obscenity in rhetorical dialogue contribute to the clarification of an issue.

SPEAKING FROM THE PODIUM

Sometimes we watch experienced orators at work on the podium expressing themselves with power and clarity, and we tend to think that it looks easy. It seems as though the words are simply flowing with complete spontaneity. When Daniel Webster made his famous "Reply to Hayne" on the floor of Congress in 1830, he was asked how he could have made such an eloquent speech on the spur of the moment. His answer was, "I've been preparing that speech all my life."

Fortunately, you do not have to spend your whole life in preparation, and no one expects you to give an eloquent presentation on the spur of the moment. You generally will have a reasonable amount of time to prepare for a speech, and you'll be able to practice before you deliver it.

ered the information you need, have organized it in a way that makes sense to you, and have practiced out loud what you want to say, you will begin to feel much more comfortable.

Preparing Note Cards

A common source of anxiety about public speaking is the fear of forgetting what you are going to say. Don't feel that you have to rely on your memory—provide yourself with materials that will assist you in remembering what you want to include in the speech. Note cards are perhaps the most reliable memory aids. You can carry them with you and use them wherever you happen to be. They are inconspicuous and do not create a distraction, since listeners are generally accustomed to speakers' using notes. You can keep them in one hand and not have to put them down when you move around or gesture. If you are working without a lectern, you can hold them at a comfortable eye level without having to lower your head and break eye contact with the audience. Another advantage is that cards don't rattle the way a sheet of paper does if your hand happens to shake a bit. When you are preparing note cards, there are a few things you should remember:

Type or write legibly. The print should be dark enough so that you will be able to see the words clearly at a glance. Underline or highlight important words. It's also a good idea to put quotation marks around direct quotes and to include the source of the quotation.

Write on only one side of the card. If you have to turn the card over, you may forget whether or not you have already covered the material on the other side. End each card with a completed thought; don't carry a sentence or a phrase over to another card.

Include only necessary words and phrases. If you write the whole speech on the note cards, you will be tempted to read rather than extemporize. Don't make your notes so detailed that the speech becomes one that is read from manuscript.

Practicing the Delivery

The hours you spend gathering material and organizing it into a workable pattern will pay off when the time comes for you to deliver the speech. Confidence results from knowing that you have done your "homework." The delivery of the speech is the part of public address that is the most gratifying because you will feel the sense of really having accomplished something. When you write an article for a magazine or newspaper, you seldom know whether or not anyone reads it. But when you give a speech, you can see the response of the people who are hearing your ideas.

An important part of the preparation for a speech is practicing the delivery. This does not mean that you have to memorize every word and every gesture. What it does mean is that you should try out the speech on someone else before you deliver it to the audience. Hearing the sound of your voice expressing the ideas will help you become familiar with them.

Try to anticipate as much as you can about the situation before you step into it. If it's possible to do so, visit the room where you will be speaking. Note the size and decor of the room, the seating arrangement, the ventilation, and anything that might create a distraction. Walk up to the front of the room and see what the perspective is from the place where you will give the speech.

When all your preparation is completed, the time will come when you will see what the audience looks like from the speaker's platform. It's then that you have a chance to apply all that you have learned and see if the theory really works for you. If it does, remember what it is that you did. If what you do falls short of your expectations, don't be disheartened; learn from the experience, and do better next time.

THE DIMENSIONS OF THE MESSAGE

You can improve your chances for success if you try to anticipate how the audience is going to receive you. From the moment you step up to the podium, your listeners will be forming in their minds an impression of the kind of person you are, how well they like you, and whether or not they are inclined to believe and accept what you have to say. The impression they receive is important because it will affect the way they react to what they see and hear. One way to analyze an audience's perception of a speaker is to look at the three dimensions that every speech contains: the primary message, the auxiliary message, and the secondary message.

Primary Message

The *primary message* is the verbal content of the speech—the words the speaker uses to express the ideas, the information, and the opinions that form the substance of the message. This is the meaning the audience would get if the channel of communication were the printed page rather than the spoken word.

Auxiliary Messages

Auxiliary messages are the dimensions to communication that can be added when the message is delivered orally. They encompass what the speaker can do deliberately to enhance the reception of the primary message. Auxiliary messages include tone of voice, vocal inflection, posture, gesture, rate of delivery, eye contact, style of dress, and other delivery techniques that the speaker can employ to reinforce what he or she is saying.

Secondary Messages

Secondary messages are messages which are projected to the audience which are not part of the speaker's plan. They are impressions created by characteristics over which the speaker has no control, such as age, sex, race, nationality, or physical appearance. They could also come about as a result of unconscious behavior patterns. Secondary messages can work to the advantage or to the disadvantage of the speaker. If they are mannerisms that indicate nervousness, uncertainty, or insincerity, they can be quite detrimental. For example, the speaker might have a distracting twitch or may be toying with a pencil. These are secondary messages that would interfere with the audience's receiving the message that the speaker wants heard. On the other hand, secondary messages can have a positive effect. The speaker may have attractive facial features, natural poise, or an empathetic expression. Qualities such as these would contribute to the audience's willingness to accept and believe what the speaker is saying.

BODY LANGUAGE

The visual impressions that we call *body language* could be in the form of auxiliary or secondary messages. Whether they are intentional or unintentional, they have a lot to do with the establishment of the speaker's credibility. Consider your own perceptions: What is it that you, as a member of the audience, like to see when you are listening to a speaker? Generally people say they observe posture that conveys a feeling of confidence, gestures that seem natural and at ease, direct eye contact, and friendly facial expressions. These characteristics are by no means proof of sincerity, but audiences do tend to make judgments based on them. We no longer teach students to rehearse gestures in front of a mirror as teachers of elocution did in previous generations. What you do on the podium should develop naturally out of your own style and personality. There are, however, some conventional behavior patterns that might be appropriate for you to consider.

Posture

The basic posture for the speaker is to stand. The reason for this is that when you stand, you are in a better position to gain and hold the attention

Gestures should be motivated and contribute naturally to the thought.

of the audience, which is of course what you want to do. Keep your weight on both feet. Don't slouch, and don't lean heavily on the desk or lectern. Avoid shifting your weight from one foot to another or pacing back and forth across the room. Try not to look as if you are tired; your audience wants to see you awake and alert, displaying a reasonable amount of vitality.

You probably will want to establish yourself behind a lectern if there is one. But remember that this piece of equipment is designed to rest your notes or manuscript on—not your body. Don't grip the sides of the lectern too tightly. A speaker with white knuckles tends to lose the confidence of the audience.

Gesture

If you are motivated to gesture, do so. Allow your hands and arms to help you communicate your ideas. It is probably better to stick with conventional speech gestures rather than to try to transmit elaborate descriptions in the air with your hands. There are a number of simple gestures that are easy to use and that will look natural to the audience: holding up fingers to indicate a number of items; drawing the hands toward the body in a welcoming motion; turning the palm out toward the audience to suggest "enough"; using a rolling motion with the hands to indicate an idea in process; and pointing to a chart or visual aid. All of these are referred to as *motivated* gestures. They are not to be inserted artificially or at random; rather they should contribute naturally to the emphasis of the thought.

Movement

Feel free to move around if there is a reason to do so. You may want to walk to the chalkboard or to a flip-chart. You might wish to change your position in order to have better visual contact with your audience. Another reason to move is to communicate intensity in the thought you want to convey. Closing the distance between you and the audience is body language for saying that the next point is very important.

Eye Contact

Maintaining eye contact with members of the audience is the speaker's way of saying, "I am aware of your presence, and I want to establish communication with you." Looking at faces is important for the sake of establishing rapport with the audience. Don't look over the top of their heads or stare at your notes; let people know that you are interested in the feedback they give you as you deliver the speech. Eye contact is one of the factors people use to determine the sincerity of a speaker. You are less likely to be trusted if the audience believes you are not willing to look them in the eye. Your eye contact is also perceived by the audience to be an indicator of your confidence level. Looking at people's faces tells them that you are sure of what you are saying.

VOCAL COMMUNICATION

While a great deal of communication occurs at the nonverbal level in public speaking, the voice is the primary instrument for conveying messages. The extent to which you will be understood depends on your ability to verbalize what you want to say. You will find that using your voice for public speaking is somewhat different from using it in ordinary conversation, particularly in terms of volume.

Volume

Beginning speakers sometimes have difficulty in determining the volume level that is required when they are speaking to a large group. Probably you are used to talking to two or three people at a time; if you use that same level of volume for twenty or thirty people, you may not be heard. If speaking up is hard for you, you will need to practice. Before the speech, have a friend stand 30 or 40 feet away from you. Deliver the speech to your friend, increasing the volume until the person is able to hear you easily. Make note of the way your voice sounds at that volume level. When the time comes for you to give the speech, you will know how loudly you have to talk. Adequate volume is one of the most fundamental requirements in public speaking. Unless people can hear what you say, your message will not be communicated.

Projection

Volume is not the only factor responsible for audibility. The extent to which you *project* your voice will also determine whether or not you can be heard. Projecting the voice means aiming the words directly at the people who are the targets of your message. The best way of doing this is to extend the sound of your voice to reach the people farthest away. That works much better than talking loudly to the people in the front row.

Pitch

The word *pitch* refers to a speaker's tone of voice. What you want to achieve is a *modulated* pitch, which means that the vocal tones rise and fall, giving emphasis to your meaning. If you are not modulating your voice, you are said to be talking in a *monotone*. This problem can be difficult to overcome, but you want to work on it because a monotone can make a speech sound dull and tedious. Practice by speaking into a tape recorder; then play back the tape and hear how your voice sounds. If you perceive that you are speaking in a monotone, go back over the written material of your speech and underline key words and phrases. Now, record the speech again, placing vocal emphasis on the items you underlined.

A related voice problem is that of a *patterned pitch*. This means that your voice is modulated, but the highs and lows are coming at regular intervals without regard for the points you want to emphasize. This problem is most likely to occur when you are reading from a book or manuscript. An audience can generally tell when you have stopped extemporizing the speech and have begun reading because the rise-and-fall patterned pitch is a dead giveaway. If you have to read portions of your speech, try to maintain the same modulated vocal inflection that you use when you extemporize.

Vocal Emphasis

Vocal emphasis is important not just for the sake of making what you say sound interesting but also for the sake of making your meaning clear. It is possible to modify the way your audience perceives your meaning without changing any of your words. For example, the following sentence could convey several different meanings, depending upon which words are emphasized:

I didn't say he stole my book.

Try speaking this sentence seven times, emphasizing a different word each time. You will find that there are seven different meanings:

1 Someone *else* said he stole my book.
2 I *deny* that I said he stole my book.
3 I might have implied it, but I didn't *say* he stole it.
4 Someone stole it, but it wasn't *he*.
5 He might have borrowed it, but he didn't *steal* it.
6 He stole someone else's book, not *mine*.
7 He stole something else, not my *book*.

From this illustration we can see that it is not only the word that conveys the meaning but the way the speaker uses the word. Words are tools that a speaker uses to communicate, just as a hammer is a tool that a carpenter uses to drive nails. The hammer by itself does not drive the nail; it's the way the hammer is used that drives the nail.

Rate of Delivery

How fast should you talk? That's a question that is hard to answer. A lot depends on your own personal style. The best thing to do is speak at a rate that is comfortable for you; however, a brisk pace works better than a slow one. A *brisk* pace is one that is rapid enough to hold the attention of the audience but not so fast that your words are running together. If you can speak rapidly and still enunciate clearly, do it. But don't sacrifice clarity for speed.

Here is some quantitative evidence you might consider: The average conversational speaking rate is about 150 words per minute; a disk jockey on a rock station will probably clip along at about 170 words per minute; a fast-talking announcer doing a commercial for a used-car company may hit 200 or 210 words per minute. Even if you could talk that fast, you probably would not want to. At that rate, words begin to become indistinguishable, and listeners are unable to comprehend what is being said. Speaking too fast also results in loss of both vocal inflection and emphasis on key words and phrases. So deliver your speech at a rate that allows you to modulate your voice and pause for the sake of emphasis.

VERBAL LANGUAGE

Your primary vehicle for communication is verbal language. If you have ever played the game of charades, you know how difficult and frustrating it is to try to convey an idea without being able to use words. For everyday interaction with people, we rely very heavily on language for communication, but we often develop careless speech habits. We frequently take verbal shortcuts when we speak, assuming that the listener will be able to fill in the blanks. For example, we may say, "You know what I mean." The other person might nod in the affirmative but not really know what we mean at all.

In public speaking, we need to break our careless speech habits because the people we are talking to don't know us well enough to guess accurately at what we mean. We need to use the right word or phrase to express what we want to say, and we must arrange our words in a sequence that people can follow.

Connecting Phrases

In an earlier chapter we looked at phrases called "transitions," which are used to help the audience follow our progression of thought leading to our conclusion. A similar kind of rhetorical device is a *connecting phrase*, which points out the relationship of one thought to another. A connecting phrase is commonly used when you want to tell the audience how a specific instance relates to a generalization. Throughout this book I have frequently used the phrase *for example* in order to tell you that what follows is an illustration of the thought that I want to convey. Here are a few other commonly used connecting phrases:

> What this means is
> This shows that
> As evidence for this we can see that
> This indicates
> As one suggestion

Just as transitions help the audience to know that it's time to move on to the next point, the connecting phrase provides a link between the abstract statement and concrete example.

EMPHASIZING KEY POINTS

Speakers sometimes seem to have the idea that everything they say will be remembered. Classroom lecturers would certainly like to believe this is true, but the results of final examinations usually do not confirm the notion. Even when a speaker's delivery is effective and the audience is attentive, about half of a fifty-minute lecture will be retained immediately after it is over; two weeks later that figure drops to 25 percent.[2] There are of course a number of variables: the importance of the information to the listeners, the extent to which they will be held responsible for the information, whether or not they are taking notes, and so on. But as a speaker, you must be realistic about how much people will be able to remember.

If your audience is going to retain only a small percentage of what you say, you have to ask yourself two questions: What are the important points in the speech, and how can I emphasize those points so they will be remembered?

Repetition

Repeating key words and important points appears to be the most effective mode of emphasis. Instructors know that this is absolutely necessary when they have reason to believe that the word or the information is being heard by students for the first time. For example, an expression that is used in the theory of argumentation and persuasion is *cognitive dissonance*. This is a term that appears frequently in professional journals, but it probably does not come up very often in everyday conversation. The two words are not really difficult to understand; *cognitive* means "knowing" and *dissonance* means "out of harmony." So *cognitive dissonance* refers to the condition that may develop when you learn something that seriously conflicts with what you had believed to be true. As a teacher, I would not expect students to be able to remember that term unless I explained what it meant and then used it several times in my lecture. Let's look at another example and see how we might use repetition in emphasizing a key piece of information:

> The population of the world will double in the next fifty years. There will be twice as many people on our planet in the year 2043.

This form is called *concentrated repetition*. The information is reinforced immediately after it is said the first time. In this case, different words were used when the data were expressed the second time, but that's not always necessary; the information could be repeated in exactly the same words. Repeating a phrase in the same words is a rhetorical device that skilled orators use to create a strong impact. Recall the words of Winston Churchill:

---

[2] Ralph G. Nichols, "Do We Know How to Listen? Practical Help in a Modern Age," *Speech Teacher*, October 1961, p. 120.

We shall defend our island, whatever the cost may be. We shall fight on the beaches. We shall fight on the landing grounds. We shall fight in the fields and in the streets; we shall fight in the hills. We shall never surrender.

Pointer Phrases

Try to make it as easy as you can for your listeners to recognize what you want them to remember. One way to do this is simply to say to them, "Now here is an important fact." We call this a *pointer phrase*; it's a device instructors often use to call attention to something that they want students to remember. In class sometime you might have heard your instructor say, "Now this information is going to be included on the final examination." That's a pointer phrase, and it's designed to get your attention. Going back to the previous example regarding population, you could preface your information in this way:

One point stands out, and this is something that will affect many people in this lifetime. Unless we can change the present trend, the population of the world will double in the next fifty years.

Be sure, however, that the statement you are pointing to is truly significant and that it is stated in such a way that it is easily remembered.

Oratorical Emphasis

The methods we have discussed so far apply to written statements as well as to spoken ones. However, there are some modes of emphasis that are available only to speakers. They include such things as dramatic pauses, vocal inflection, changes in volume, and the use of gestures. As a speaker, you have access not only to verbal communication but also to all the methods of nonverbal communication as well.

Visual Reinforcement

Human beings probably first learned to talk by using visual aids. When you show an object and make a sound, you establish a connection between the word and the thing. Once that connection is made, it's no longer necessary to show the object. Children learn to talk in the same way. As our vocabulary grows, we are able to rely more and more on language for communication, but we know that visual reinforcement is still a powerful teaching tool. If you want something to stick in your listeners' minds, give them a picture as well as a verbal description. Modern learning theories tell us that people store events in two ways—through visual images and through verbal codes.[3] The more vivid you can make the visual image, the more likely it is that the idea will be remembered. Not every point you want to make can be projected pictorially, but when you have access to visuals that illustrate your words, use them. Here again, the principle you want to remember is that your chances for success in public speaking have a lot to do with your ability to make it as easy as you can for the audience to comprehend the message and then retain it after they have heard it.

RESPONDING TO QUESTIONS

Most of the time your communication with the audience does not end with the conclusion of your speech; it's very likely that there will be a question period afterward. This is a time you should welcome as a speaker, because when the audience asks questions, you can learn what they were thinking while you were talking. The interaction that takes place at this time provides an opportunity for you to clarify any misunderstandings and to elaborate on points of interest. If the topic is controversial, you will get some insight into the objections people have to your thesis or to your arguments. Be sure to communicate to your audience that you are interested in their reactions and welcome their comments. Regard their questions as evidence that they were involved in what you were saying and want to extend the dialogue. For the most part the responses you make to questions will have to be spontaneous, but there are some things you can do to prepare:

Know Your Subject   It is at this time that your audience will not only have a chance to clarify any points of confusion but will also be able to find out if you really know what you are talking about. You should be able to add new information and use different examples in your replies, so that you aren't simply restating what you have already said.

Anticipate Questions   If you are well-prepared, there should be few questions that take you by surprise. If your subject matter is controversial, try to think of what objections there might be to the claims you are making. Don't let the audience believe you have been caught off guard by a challenging question. Make them think that you welcome the opportunity to clarify your point.

---

[3] Albert Bandura, *Social Learning Theory*, Prentice-Hall, Englewood Cliffs, N.J., 1977, p. 59.

Direct Your Answers to the Whole Audience   First of all, make sure everyone has heard the question; if you have any doubt about this, repeat the question so the whole audience can hear it and have the questioner confirm your paraphrase. By doing this, you make sure you understand what the questioner is asking, and you also buy a little time that you can use for thinking about how you are going to respond. When you give your answer, make sure that everyone knows you are addressing the whole audience. Remember, your response to the questions is part of the speech.

Be Succinct   Don't make the mistake of launching into another speech in response to the first question; that has the effect of discouraging others from participating. Answer the question directly, but make it brief. If the question calls for a more detailed answer, or if it is off the topic of the speech, invite the person to speak to you at the end of the presentation so you can discuss the issue further.

Encourage Involvement   The question period should move rapidly and involve as many people as there is time for. There will always be those who will try to make speeches of their own from the floor, or who will ask you one question after another. Don't let that happen. If a question starts getting too lengthy or has too many parts to it, you may have to interrupt. Do it politely, give the best answer you can, and then move on to someone else. If you get caught in a dialogue with one person, you will lose the attention of the rest.

Maintain Control   The question period is part of your presentation; it is not a group discussion. You should try to get lots of people involved, but be sure they don't take the floor away from you and start addressing questions to each other. This can easily happen if you allow long questions or fail to reply to each one. Sometimes a person will make a comment that is not in the form of a question. Treat it like a question and make some sort of response to acknowledge that you have heard.

Know When to Stop   Since the question period is an important part of your speech, be sure you allow enough time for it. The length of a question period depends entirely on the circumstances. Often there are time limitations—other speakers may be scheduled, or your audience may be on their lunch hour. If your time is not restricted, you will have to judge for yourself how long to allow questions to continue. Probably there will be a moderator who will let the audience know that the time is up. When that happens, have a final comment in mind that you can use to bring closure to the presentation.

ASSESSING YOUR PROGRESS

After you have made your first speech, you are in a position to assess your progress. This is a good time to stop and reflect on what you have learned so far from the text, from the lecture material you have had in class, and from your actual experience of speaking. Review the criteria that were suggested in the first chapter, and see how well you think you have observed them. You may have received some feedback on your speech from the other students in the class, and you probably also got a grade from your instructor. All of that is very helpful, but the important thing is for you to be satisfied with your own progress. Don't let a speaking opportunity go by without learning something from the experience.

EXERCISE

Public speaking is a lot less difficult when you know what information your audience is interested in hearing. A good way to practice is to provide your listeners with a set of questions that you know you can answer. As a preparatory exercise, write three or four questions on small slips of paper and give them to several members of the class. Have those people sit in the back of the room while you stand at the front. The questions should be open-ended so that you have an opportunity to elaborate rather than giving just a simple yes or no answer. Number the questions so that they are asked in a logical sequence. This exercise will give you practice in phrasing questions, organizing material, speaking extemporaneously, and talking loud enough to be heard. In responding to a question give a complete answer, but don't ramble. When you have finished your thought, drop your voice so another person can ask the next question. Here are examples of questions you might want people to ask on the subject of family counseling:

1 What are the requirements in this state for becoming a marriage and family counselor?

2 How does a person receive the kind of experience needed to obtain a counseling certificate?

3 What career opportunities are there for a person who has the certificate?

4 What are some of the problems people have when they come to a marriage and family counselor?

5 How successful can a counselor expect to be in helping families deal with their problems?

You might notice that the questions above appear to be similar to what you might find as the main headings in the outline of a speech. You are right; they are. The only difference is that they are phrased in the form of questions. When you prepare your next outline, you might consider using this technique. There is nothing wrong with writing your main headings as questions.

QUESTIONS FOR REVIEW

1 What do we mean by *standard English*? Why is it recommended for most public speaking situations? What is the disadvantage of using slang expressions?

2 What effect might the use of obscenity have on an audience?

3 Who made the "Reply to Hayne" on the floor of Congress in 1830?

4 What do we mean by *impromptu speaking*? What are some ways you can "prepare" for an impromptu speech?

5 What are the advantages and disadvantages of memorizing a speech or reading it from manuscript?

6 How does an extemporaneous speech differ from an impromptu speech? Why is the extemporaneous speech generally the mode of delivery that is emphasized in most public speaking classes?

7 Explain the meaning of primary, auxiliary, and secondary messages.

8 What do we mean by *motivated gestures*?

9 Why is it important for a speaker to maintain eye contact with the audience?

10 Besides making the speech more interesting to listen to, what else is accomplished by vocal inflection?

11 How fast does the average person speak? About how fast can a really rapid talker speak?

12 What do we mean by *connecting phrases*? How do they differ from transitional phrases?

13 What are four ways to put emphasis on a word or phrase?

14 How does concentrated repetition differ from distributed repetition?

15 What is meant by a *pointer phrase*?

16 What kinds of devices fall under the heading of "oratorical emphasis"?

17 How can you prepare for the question period of a speech?

CHAPTER 9

SPEAKING WITH VISUALS

Confucius was probably right when he said that a picture is worth a thousand words. In any case, television advertisers who invest heavily in the visual media wager hundreds of millions of dollars every year that it is true, and people who are involved in making business presentations would do well to follow that example. The fact is that there are many things that cannot be communicated in words. How could a fashion designer describe to an audience of buyers what the latest Paris styles were without using pictures or models? How could an architect convey to a group of contractors what a building was supposed to look like without showing them drawings? Words alone are just not adequate for important presentations that require the audience to reproduce in their own minds the same picture that you have in yours.

HIGH-STAKES PRESENTATIONS

With so much emphasis being placed on giving speeches in the classroom, you might begin to think that the purpose of learning the skills of public address is entirely academic. The fact is that your most important speeches probably will be given after you leave college. You might find yourself in the position of having to make a presentation to an influential group such as a city council, or possibly your opportunity to speak will come on the job when a proposal needs to be made to a senior management–level committee. The stakes after college are likely to be much higher than they are now, and the success of your presentation could have a significant effect on your career.

Everything that has been said so far in this text applies to real-life situations as well as those that occur in the classroom. There is, however, a difference that we need to take into consideration in regard to the way you will be evaluated. In the classroom your instructor is going to give you a grade based on how well you fulfill the assignment, prepare the outline, develop the topic, and deliver the speech. In a real-life situation, the people in the audience are the ones who make the evaluation, and they are going to base their assessment on how useful the information is to them and how clear you are able to make it. Let's look at effective ways to proceed when it's really important that your listeners get the full impact of your message.

Speaking to a Specific Audience

We have already discussed the importance of designing a speech for a *general* audience, but when you prepare a speech for a *specific* audience, it is necessary for you to sharpen the focus of the topic even more. In a classroom you have a general audience composed of people with many different interests and levels of comprehension. The material you present to them cannot be highly technical because they would not have the background to understand it. But an audience that has assembled because of a specific interest will expect you to go beyond what they already know and present material in greater depth and detail. If the speech is to be useful to them, they must be able to connect what you tell them to what they already know, and they must be able to remember what they hear. It may be that the purpose of your presentation is to get the audience to approve your recommendation, to buy what you are selling, or to take action based on your information. That's a real challenge, particularly when you may be limited to only twenty or thirty minutes. What we're talking about here is a speech that looks and sounds like a professional presentation.

A speech to a general audience—one that would be appropriate for the classroom—might describe how a network of computers can perform a variety of tasks in a business office, but if you were speaking to a group of people who already use computers in their places of business, you would have to go into more depth and detail. For example, you might make a presentation on a particular program application that is designed for a specific accounting function, or recommend a way to provide security for confidential information that is stored in a computer. Before you make this kind of speech, there are several matters you have to consider:

- Does the audience have the technical background to understand the new information that you plan to present?
- Is it enough for the audience merely to understand the information, or must they be able to retain it and apply it?
- Do you have all the facilities you need to make it possible for the audience to visualize what you explain and to remember what you tell them?
- Will your explanation be sufficient for the audience to learn, or will they need to have "hands-on experience"?
- Are materials available for the audience to review after the presentation is over?
- Is it necessary for you to know whether or not the audience has learned what you have told them?

The Tools of the Trade

There are times when you may have to be more than just a speaker; you might need to be a teacher. Under those circumstances you must anticipate what your listeners require in order for them to be able to learn. Holding an audience's attention is one thing, but now we are adding a new and much more difficult dimension to public speaking—getting people to comprehend fully and *retain* what they have heard. To do this it is necessary that you learn to use all the tools of the trade. Language will still be your principal means of communication, but often you will find that it is not enough.

Physical Objects Of all the visual aids you can use, the object itself is perhaps the best. To teach a person to swim requires that you have a body of water; to help someone play the guitar, you must let them hold the instrument; to provide instruction on how to use a piece of software, you will need to demonstrate on a computer. In all these cases, verbal description alone is not sufficient, and there is no point in going through the motions of teaching unless the listener is able to learn. There may be occasions when it is not possible to produce the real physical object itself, and the speaker may have to rely on a model. This is a technique that might be used by an engineer who is describing a plan for a new suspension bridge or a dentist who is explaining how to do a root canal. The model helps the listener visualize what the speaker is saying, and we know that visualization is an important adjunct to learning.

Two-Dimensional Pictures If you can't get the object itself and are not able to obtain a model of it, you can use two-dimensional visuals in the form of photographs, drawings, sketches, paintings, cartoons, diagrams, exploded or cutaway diagrams, bar charts (Figure 9–1), line graphs (Figure

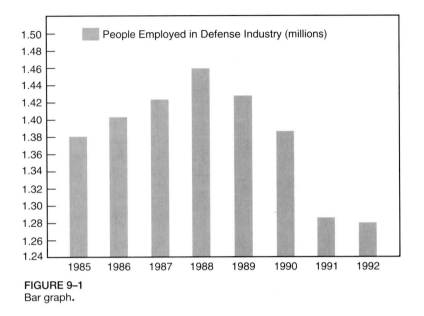

FIGURE 9–1
Bar graph.

9–2), pie charts (Figure 9–3), blueprints, maps, key words (Figure 9–4), or any combination of those listed. Illustrations in color are best, but black and white will do. They can be displayed by means of computer projection, overhead transparencies, slide projection, opaque projection, movie camera, or video screen. And, of course, a method that does not require electronic equipment is simply to mount the visuals on the wall or on an easel. The important thing is that they be big enough and clear enough for the audience to see.

WHAT VISUALS CAN ACCOMPLISH

Using visuals for important presentations will help you transform the casual speech into one that has a professional appearance. Consider the visuals you need for your speech in the same way you regard information and evidence. If there were a particular fact that you had to have to support your position, you would need to find it. By the same token, if there is a visual you need in order to make your point understandable, you will need to create it. Not every speech requires visuals, but if you try to do without them when they are needed, you will leave gaping holes in your presentation. Let's look at some of the ways that visuals can contribute to your talk.

Overhead transparencies help the audience retain information.

series of screen displays, arranging them in the sequence you want, and then projecting them as you would when running a slide show. A hand-held device allows you to preview the next visual before you display it, and also gives you a palm-size image of your notes to help you recall what you want to say. You can also set the timing between images and have the program run by itself while you make the commentary.

Slides and Transparencies

For the speaker who wants to use visuals but does not feel comfortable around computers, slides and transparencies give the most "bang for the buck." They are effective in gaining and holding attention and contribute significantly to the impact of the message.

The content of the slide or transparency can be just about anything you want it to be. The slide projector is probably a better piece of equipment to use for displaying color photographs, although transparencies can also be used for that purpose. The overhead projector lends itself effectively to the display of charts, graphs, lists, diagrams, and key words, but slides can be made to do those things as well. Here are the generic functions of slides and transparencies:

• They can project an image on a screen large enough so that all members of the audience can see the picture at the same time.
• They work equally well for large or small audiences.
• The pictures can be changed easily and quickly either by an operator or by the person who is giving the speech.
• The speaker can call attention to items on the screen with a pointer.
• The speaker can be facing the audience while describing the image or changing the picture.

Transparencies and slides each have characteristics of their own that may cause you to select one medium over the other: Transparencies have the advantage of being flexible. You can change the sequence more easily than you can when you are using slides; the room does not have to be totally darkened in order to get clear resolution on the screen; you can call attention to items in the picture by pointing on the transparency itself; you can write on the transparency with a marking pencil; and you can conceal part of the material on the transparency with a blank card or sheet of paper until you are ready to have the audience see it.

Slides have the advantage of producing high-quality images. Photographs can be projected with a realistic, three-dimensional look; the color in slides gives the presentation a highly professional appearance; the projected images can be changed quickly and easily, moving forward or backward with the press of a button; and the speaker can operate the equipment without the aid of an assistant.

SPEAKING WITH TRANSPARENCIES

Always make sure that the visuals you work with in making a presentation are set out in a way that facilitates the logistics of their use; you don't want to have to hunt for something when you are under pressure. The transparencies should have cardboard borders for easy handling, they should be titled, and they should be stacked in order.

• Have the first transparency lined up on the projector and in focus so that when you turn the machine on it will appear without delay.

• Cover with cardboard any part you don't want displayed immediately. During the presentation, slide the cardboard down to reveal the figures or diagrams you want the audience to see. This technique will give focus to the audience's attention.

• Display the transparency long enough for the audience to assimilate the information, but don't leave it there when you have gone on to another point.

• Have some comment about every transparency you display, so the audience will know what you have in mind. Don't expect the visual aid to speak for itself; your responsibility as the presenter is to help the audience understand the significance of what you are showing them.

• Be familiar enough with the material on the transparency that you can direct your attention to the audience rather than to the screen.

SPEAKING WITH SLIDES

Be sure you know how the equipment works. Familiarize yourself with the kind of projector you will be using in the presentation. The best equipment would consist of a carousel projector with remote controls. Load the carousel yourself (slides go in upside down and backwards), and run through them to make sure they are in the right sequence. Experiment with the switches on your remote control unit. You will be able to go backward and forward; you may have to focus manually unless that function is automatic on the projector.

• Position the projector to accommodate the audience. Make sure the slides will be displayed so that everyone will be able to see. Try to avoid the "keystone" effect by keeping the projector on a straight line with the screen. Select a place where you can stand so that you are not blocking anyone's view. And be sure you have a cord long enough to reach the electrical outlet.

• Practice using a pointer. There may be occasions when you want to call attention to a particular item on the display. The conventional speaker's pointer may work well enough, but if you are some distance from the screen, a light-beam pointer might be necessary. If you have never used one before, try it out before you confront your audience.

• Consider how you will use your notes. Remember that the lights are going to be out when you show the slides. In a darkened room you may not be able to see your note cards. It may be that you will not have to use them at all because the slides themselves will help you recall what you want to say. But if you do have to use notes, provide a small light for yourself at your speaker's lectern.

• Designate a person to turn the lights on and off, and another person to start the slide projector. Remember that you are going to be in the front of the room facing the audience and you don't want to leave your listeners in darkness with nothing to see or hear.

• Pace your presentation. There are too many variables to make a recommendation on how long to show each slide; you will have more to say about some than others. But keep in mind the attention span of your audiences and the number of slides you intend to include. Averaging four slides a minute, you'll be able to show 120 slides in a half-hour presentation. Remember that after the first twenty minutes the attention of the audience begins to decline, and they are sitting in a darkened room; don't let them fall asleep.

Integrating Slides into the Presentation

The effectiveness of the slide presentation depends to a large extent on your ability to work the visuals into the content of the message. Basically your presentation should be *content-driven.* In other words, select the visuals to illustrate what you want to say, rather than devise things to say about the visuals that happen to be available to you.

When you are planning the presentation, think of the visuals as part of the rhetorical dialogue, not as disconnected entities. All too often I have seen people give a speech, and then show their slides as though the two were separate presentations. Prepare the speech as you normally would with an attention statement, a purpose statement, main ideas, supporting information, and conclusion. The visuals you use need to fit into the structure of your speech.

Work out the logistics of the speech. That means have a clear idea of the physical sequence starting from the time you are introduced. Every situation is different, so there are no immutable rules; however, you may find that a few guidelines are useful.

1 Begin by establishing your own personal contact with the audience. Use some introductory material to get their attention and provide them with enough orientation information that they will know what you are going to talk about and what you will be showing them.

2 When you are ready for the slides, signal the people who have previously been designated to control the light switch and start the projector. Don't try to do those things yourself.

3 Control the slide changing with your remote switching device. You can do that easily with your thumb. (Make sure you have the right button so you go forward instead of backward.) Have something to say about each slide that is projected.

4 When the last slide has been shown, have the lights turned back on and the projector turned off. Don't finish the speech in darkness. Let the audience see you as you are delivering your conclusion.

As you can see, there are some logistical complications in making a slide presentation and more things to think about than there are in the unaided speech. You will need to do some planning and make advance preparation, but the impact on your audience will be significantly greater.

DO-IT-YOURSELF VISUALS

An oral explanation, in my opinion, is more effective than a written one. There are, however, some advantages to information that appears on the printed page. Complex material, particularly that which contains a great many names and numbers, may require some study on the part of the receiver. Sometimes oral presentations do not allow enough time for the listener to assimilate the material, and the message does not get thoroughly imprinted. When you believe that your audience may need to review what you have told them after the presentation, you can provide a handout sheet for them. If you want them to follow along while you are providing the explanation, give it to them in advance. But most teachers will tell you that it's a better idea to give your information orally; then distribute the handout sheets.

Not all visuals need to be prepared in advance. There are times when you may want to create the visuals as you deliver the speech. The best example of such an occasion is when you are conducting a brainstorming session. You have several choices in selecting your equipment:

• **The chalkboard.** This is the old standby—possibly the world's first visual aid. It works well enough if you don't mind chalk dust on your clothes. I'm not fond of it for professional presentations because it looks a bit funky and old-fashioned, and tends to create a "classroom" atmosphere. It is also restrictive in terms of space, and your material cannot be saved.

• **The whiteboard.** This is a better choice. It eliminates the chalk dust problem and gives a more professional appearance to the presentation. However, there is still the restriction of space and the problem of having to erase your material.

The flip-chart can be used instead of note cards and can help the speaker as well as the audience.

- **The flip-chart.** This is perhaps the best choice. You have enough pages so that you are not going to run out of space, and you don't have to erase the material. The pages can be torn off and turned over to a secretary to be recorded, or possibly pinned up around the room so that the participants have a visual record of the ideas that have been generated.

The flip-chart has other advantages as well as those just mentioned. I like to use this piece of equipment as a substitute for note cards. What I do ahead of time is put my key words and main ideas on the pages in the sequence that I want to follow. As I move through the speech, I simply turn the pages—just as though I am revealing my notes to the audience as I go through the speech. The advantage of this technique is that I can give my full attention to the audience without the need to be looking at something which they can't see. When I look at the page on the flip-chart, they can see it too. Then, with my felt-tip pen, I can highlight items that I want to emphasize.

Desk-Top Visuals

As we observed earlier, there are times when the best visual aid is the object itself or a representative model. Small pieces of equipment or artifacts can be held up or passed around if your audience is not too big. There are a number of ways you can display small, lightweight objects. The important thing is that they be visible to the audience while you are talking.

- Pin items to a corkboard.
- Hang objects from overhead clips.
- Place felt cutouts on a flannel board.
- Prop posters on an easel.

Don't put yourself in the awkward position of having to hold a large visual aid in front of you for a long period of time; either prop it or have someone else hold it. For a small audience, a desk-top easel can be used in the same way as a flip-chart. A loose-leaf binder that can be mounted on a stand is very convenient. It can also be carried easily and set up quickly.

Whenever you use visual aids, you need to take into consideration the particular circumstances of the speaking occasion. What works for a small audience may not work for a large one. The same is true in regard to your own voice and appearance. Let's consider what equipment is needed in order to extend your speech to a larger audience.

MICROPHONES AND CAMERAS

The presentation you give to a small group should work well enough without amplification, but when you are speaking to a large audience, you may need a public-address (PA) system. As the speaker, the only thing you should have to be concerned about is the way you use the microphone, because the technicians will monitor the volume control. There's no need to be intimidated by a PA system; all it will do is amplify the sound so you can be heard without your having to raise your voice to an uncomfortable level. Use enough volume so that you can be heard 20 or 30 feet away, and the amplifier will do the rest. Just remember a few techniques:

- Speak into the microphone from about 4 to 6 inches away and at a slight angle. Try to keep the distance as constant as possible. You will know that the system is working when you hear the sound reverberation that is created by the amplifier.
- While the microphone is turned on, don't make any muttering or whispering sounds to yourself or to anyone else that you don't want the audience to hear. Microphones are sensitive and will pick up even low-volume noises.
- Handling the microphone will cause it to rattle. If it needs to be adjusted, let someone else do it for you. If you have to adjust it yourself, grasp it firmly, move it, let go, and then start talking. Never tap on the microphone or blow into it.

Radio Microphones

If your speech is being carried on a radio broadcasting station, apply the same microphone techniques that were described for the use of public-address systems. The only difference is that you will not hear the sound of your voice amplified. There are two very important things to remember when your speech is being broadcast:

1 Don't start talking until you are given the cue. That will come in the form of a red light going on or a director's hand pointing at you. Once you have been given the cue, start right off with your first word, not a nonverbal sound like "uh." And *never* begin by saying, "Are we on?"

2 As you get to the end of the speech, the director will give you a "wind-it-up" signal by making a circular hand motion in the air. This signal doesn't mean stop abruptly in the middle of a sentence; it means you are to finish what you are saying and drop your voice to indicate that you are through. Don't ignore the signal; there is hardly any point in continuing to speak when the mike is turned off.

Television Cameras

The use of television has become so prevalent in our society that it is difficult to avoid. The medium is no longer the exclusive preserve of the big networks. Local stations are able to take portable cameras into almost any situation to provide news coverage. Schools and colleges commonly use television for instructional purposes; industry, too, uses it as a training tool; and home units are becoming more and more popular. Again, some techniques are important for effective use of the television medium.

• Look at the person to whom you are talking. If that person is the viewer, look at the camera. If there are other people on camera with you, talk to them. Never talk to the monitor screen regardless of how tempting it may be to look at yourself.

• Avoid sudden or unpredictable movements. If you stand up quickly or walk off to one side, you will move right out of the picture. If you move suddenly toward or away from the camera, you will go out of focus.

• Pay attention to your posture whether standing or sitting. Avoid slouching, scratching your head, tapping your foot, and other ungainly and unnecessary movements that distract the viewer. Remember that those mannerisms will be magnified because the television screen is able to bring you up close to the audience.

All the electronic media should be viewed by the speaker not as a threat but as an enhancement of the communication art, providing an opportunity to deliver the message more clearly to more people.

PUTTING IT ALL TOGETHER

Modern technology has made public speaking a great deal more complex than it was in Aristotle's time—or in the time of Confucius. You can still give speeches the old-fashioned way, relying completely on your unaided voice and your personal image. In fact, that may be what you will be doing most of the time when you have the opportunity to speak, but be sure you know that audio and visual aids are available to you. Don't feel that you are restricted to any one particular kind; you can use a number of those that have been mentioned in combination. Think in terms of the effect that you want to create and what it is that you want to have stand out in the mind of the audience. Then select the object or the equipment that will do the job most effectively for you. Actually, it may be that Confucius underestimated—a picture could be worth a good deal more than a thousand words.

EXERCISE

Find one example to illustrate each type of visual aid listed below. Stand in front of the class, display the visuals, and make a short comment about each one. Be sure you plan the logistics: Figure out how you are going to mount the visuals and where you are going to stand when you display them.

- A printed list of key words to indicate steps in a process
- A bar chart, a pie chart, or a line graph showing percentages
- A map of a geographic area that you can describe
- A painting, diagram, poster, or large photograph

Make sure that all the visuals you display are large enough to be seen. Use stiff paper or poster board so they will stand upright on an easel or chalk tray. Use a dark-colored felt-tip pen for printing and drawing. If you have projection equipment, you can display your visuals on slides or transparencies.

QUESTIONS FOR REVIEW

1 In a real-life situation (as opposed to a classroom) what will probably be the audience's main criteria for evaluating a speaker?

2 When your speech is being given for a specific audience rather than for a general audience, what changes might you have to make in the purpose and in the content?

3 What new challenge is added to a presentation on the occasions when you have to be a teacher rather than just a speaker?

4 What are some of the ways visuals can be displayed? In terms of the audience's perception, what are the most important criteria for the display of visuals?

5 Why would you want to use visuals in a speech? What are some things they can accomplish?

6 What do we mean when we say that visuals communicate more *succinctly* than words?

7 What do we mean by *appealing to aesthetic senses?*

8 In addition to helping the audience understand and retain the message, how do visuals help the speaker in making the presentation?

9 Why is the persona of the speaker still the most important element in speechmaking? What can the speaker do that visuals cannot do?

10 What kind of visuals can you display using computer projection? What advantage does a computer-projected image have over a standard transparency?

11 What piece of equipment is probably best for displaying color photographs?

12 What piece of equipment would you probably want to use if you had several graphs, charts, and lists to display but did not want to be confined to arranging them in a particular order?

13 What advantages does a flip-chart have over a chalkboard?

14 What is the value of handouts? At what point in the presentation should they be distributed?

15 How should visuals be integrated into a speech?

CHAPTER 10

SPEAKING OCCASIONS

Every task of any complexity requires that you have a conceptual understanding of what the actual practice entails. When you applied for a driver's license, it was necessary for you to learn the rules of the road by reading the manual. After that, you were given a learner's permit, and before you received your license, you had to demonstrate that you were able to handle an automobile on city streets. You were probably capable of becoming a driver without going through that process, but the mistakes you might have made along the way could have been extremely costly. A better plan is to learn the concept, practice the operation, and then begin applying what you know. This methodology is just as relevant to public speaking as it is to driving a car. Once you have learned the theory, you are in a good position to begin practicing by giving short speeches for special occasions.

THE MINISPEECH

The expression *giving a speech* has an ominous sound to it. It suggests the need to spend hours in the library researching a topic, writing an outline, making notes, and practicing the delivery. A long speech certainly may require all of that, but many times a talk you are called upon to give will be short and may need very little preparation. The principles that have been described so far in this text are still going to apply; the only difference will be that what you say can be compacted into what we might call a "minispeech." While that term sounds easier and a lot less demanding, there are still a great many people who make contorted efforts to avoid making even the shortest announcements if there are more than a dozen people listening. Having a willingness to speak to groups makes it possible for you to provide a valuable service to others, and at the same time contribute to your own personal growth, self-esteem, and professional advancement. Let's look at a few of the opportunities you might have to make a mini-speech.

Giving a Toast

Making a toast at a wedding or any special occasion is a long-standing tradition. To do this well it is necessary that you have a close connection to the people being toasted and that you are familiar with the values of those who are to share in the toast. The most important element in this kind of speaking occasion is sincerity. The toast may have a humorous twist to it, but it also needs to be seriously affirming, with perhaps a touch of sentimentality. It does not have to be elaborately developed; it can be a single thought. However, you still need to gain the attention of the audience, identify the subject, express the main idea, and end with a concluding statement just as you do in any other speech. Dave Fulmer has good advice to give in his book *A Gentleman's Guide to Toasting.*

> If seated at a table, stand when offering your toast. Don't raise your glass or drink when you're the one being toasted; it's like applauding for yourself. If you're uncomfortable not doing anything, as soon as the toast is completed, raise your glass and say, "Thank you—and here's to all of you." Don't toast the guest of honor before the host has the opportunity. Avoid signaling for quiet by rapping on a glass with a spoon—the results could be shattering.[1]

Expressing a Word of Thanks

Special occasions such as large dinner parties, business conventions, class reunions, weekend workshops, or day-long seminars require a great deal of planning and preparation on the part of the people who organize them. Often that work is done on a volunteer basis, and the individuals who put in their time need to be recognized for their efforts. At some point during the occasion, either at the beginning or at the end, take the initiative to give a word of thanks to those who made the event possible. When you do this, make sure you get the attention of everyone, have the people who are receiving acknowledgment stand, know all of them by name, and make sure you don't leave out anyone. After you have said the words to express

---

[1] Dave Fulmer, *A Gentleman's Guide to Toasting,* Oxmoor House, Lynchburg, Tenn., 1990, p. 13.

your thanks, start the applause so that others in the audience will follow suit. The main thing is that you want the ones being honored to feel affirmed.

Making an Award for a Notable Achievement

This is a short occasional speech that you might need to give when someone has made an achievement such as winning a tournament, receiving a scholarship, or graduating with honors. Again, you would start by getting the attention of the group; then call up the one who is to receive the award and have the person stand beside you. Next, describe the reason the person is being honored and what he or she was required to accomplish. You might want to give a bit of the history of the award itself so that people will appreciate the significance of the achievement. After that, tell the audience about the qualifications of the person receiving the award. Make the presentation short and be sure that the focus is on the recipient rather than on yourself.

Announcing a Coming Event

If you are a member of a club or an organization, you know that there are many occasions when announcements have to be made about coming events. You may wonder why such an effort is necessary. It seems as though we should simply be able to post a notice on the bulletin board and let people read it for themselves. The fact of the matter is that fliers or written memos do not have the same impact as the oral message. A speaker can generate interest and communicate a sense of importance that cannot be conveyed effectively by the printed word. To announce a coming event, make sure you have in your mind everything the audience needs to know. If you have any concern about forgetting, write the details down on a note card before you begin. Use the same methodology that the journalist uses: Tell *what* the event is, *who* is invited, *why* it is important, *how much* it will cost, *where* it is to be held, *when* it will start, and *how long* it will last. The audience might also want to know if it's a benefit for a cause, how often it will be repeated, and if they need to get tickets in advance. Try to be as well informed as you can, and be sure to convey enthusiasm. After you have made the announcement, you can provide reinforcement by posting a written notice or giving handout sheets to people who are interested.

Calling for Volunteers

Public speaking is an important part of leadership because it's a skill that makes it possible for you to mobilize other people to support a cause. You may be a creative and hard-working person, but if you can't recruit others to help, you will be limited in the amount you are able to accomplish. Getting people involved has multiple benefits. You as the initiator receive the help you need, the project gets completed, the burden of the task is distributed so that no one person is overloaded, and the people recruited receive the satisfaction of being part of a team effort. A mistake you want to avoid when you are asking for volunteers is to be apologetic about it. You are, of course, requesting that people take time away from their busy schedules, but you have to be sure in your mind that what you are having them do is worthwhile. Begin by describing the task that needs to be done and what end results you expect to achieve; let the group know what skills are needed and how much time and effort is going to be involved. Be sure you are realistic. Don't say it's going to be easy if it's not. Don't minimize the skill level that is required if what you want is quality work. Let them know how firm a commitment they are making and the extent to which you are counting on them. When you get your volunteers, write down names and phone numbers and make a follow-up call without delay.

Introducing a Speaker

When you are called on to introduce a speaker, you need to consider that you are performing two functions: You are giving a brief speech of your own, but you are also part of the presentation that is to be made by the major speaker. Your own speech must have an introduction, a main idea, specific details, and a conclusion; at the same time you must remember that what you say is designed primarily to help the person you are introducing gain the attention of the audience. Your most important purpose is to pave the way for the main event by generating interest in the topic and establishing the credibility of the speaker. Here are some ways you can accomplish that:

- Begin by welcoming the audience and letting them know you are glad they could come.
- Relieve the speaker of any mundane responsibilities such as asking the audience not to smoke and telling them where the bathrooms are.
- When you start your introduction, use the speaker's full name and title; make sure your pronunciation is correct.
- Tell what position the speaker currently holds and what recent accomplishments he or she has made that pertain to the subject matter of the speech.
- Relate a bit of personal history and perhaps an anecdote that has endearing qualities. You want to portray the speaker as being a likable person.

- Don't say, "Our speaker today needs no introduction." It's trite and it may not be true.
- Don't exaggerate the speaker's wisdom or capabilities; it will embarrass the person and may cause the audience to become disappointed.
- Conclude your introduction with a cue for the audience to applaud. You can say simply, "Please welcome Mr. So-and-so," and then yield the podium.

Always remember when you are giving a speech of introduction that it's not you who is the featured attraction. You may be very interested in the topic and perhaps even know a lot about it, but be sure you don't preempt the speaker's remarks by making your own editorial comments about the subject matter. Doing that is intrusive and may in fact conflict with the speaker's point of view.

SPEAKING TO A COMMITTEE

Learning how to function effectively as a member of a discussion or decision-making group is an area of speech communication that is different from public speaking; however, there are certain elements of similarity. Normally, you would not need to make the same kind of preparation for a meeting that you would when you are going to be a principal speaker. But there might be occasions when you have specific thoughts to contribute and you don't want to take up a great deal of the time of the other members. For example, you may be about to embark on a special project, and you need the approval of the members of the committee before you proceed. Rather than relying on your ability to speak in an impromptu fashion, it's a good idea to make a few notes beforehand. By doing that, you will be sure to include all the details that you want the other members to know, and you will have the ideas arranged in a logical sequence. There are some differences, of course, between group discussion and public speaking. One is that you will do your speaking sitting down rather than standing up. That has both advantages and disadvantages. The advantage is that you may feel less nervous; the disadvantage is that other members of the committee will probably interrupt you from time to time with their own comments, and that may throw you off stride. If you stand when you speak, you are sending a nonverbal message that says, "I have the floor and I expect to be heard all the way through before you respond." Sitting down says, "We are communicating on an equal basis, and I invite you to speak if you want to comment on what I am saying."

There is another important difference between public speaking and group discussion: Public speaking is an individual endeavor in which you arrive at a conclusion that is based on your own thought and research; you

Being prepared when you make a report to a committee will save the members valuable time.

then defend the position you have taken with the best evidence and reason you can produce. Group discussion is thought *in process.* That means you come to the meeting with a tentative thesis, but you know that your conclusion is subject to change on the basis of the input you receive from other members of the committee. You may prepare your presentation to a committee in the same way you prepare for a public speech, but after hearing what you say, the other members may want you to make some changes in the plans you have for your project. At that point you would have to make a choice to either accept their recommendations or continue to argue for your original plan.

THE INFORMATIVE PRESENTATION

The complexity of our society places a heavy burden on committees and individuals who have authority in a broad area of responsibility and who need to make policy decisions based on specific information. When neither the chairperson nor the members of the committee feel that they have the expertise to make such a decision, a specialist may be called in to provide the information that is needed. You may be the person selected to make a presentation that serves this purpose, not because of your skill in public speaking, but because of your knowledge of the subject matter. Your effectiveness in fulfilling this task may have a lot to do with the committee's making a good decision; it may also have a bearing on your own career and whether or not you are called back on another occasion to perform a similar function.

The informative presentation may have a controversial element, and you might have a particular bias as to what you think the decision should be. The chances are that you will be asked to make a recommendation, but you must remember that ultimately it is the committee's decision and not your own. Your job is to tell your audience what they need to know in order for them to make an informed choice, and that means explaining to them any possible disadvantages they may have to confront if your recommendation is accepted. If you gloss over the obstacles, you might be called on later to explain why you had not brought them up in the first place.

Let's say, for example, that the decision to be made is whether or not to expand and improve the company's printing and duplicating facilities. Assume that you are a technical specialist in this field and have been asked to describe the capabilities of certain pieces of equipment that are under consideration. You might have personal preferences of your own, but it's important that you set those aside and take into account the needs of the company that is going to invest in the equipment, the personnel, and the space. You would need to know the quality of the work that the company expects, and what their present requirements are in terms of volume. You should also have some insight into the growth potential of the company and what their needs might be in future years. That's a big order. Let's further assume that you have thirty minutes to make your presentation and answer questions, that you will be talking to a group of busy and highly paid people, and that you want to utilize their time as efficiently as possible.

Planning Your Strategy

1 Start planning your presentation by talking with people who understand the goals of the company and the standards of quality that are expected. Learn as much as you can about the budgetary limitations, the operating skills of the personnel, the maintenance facilities that are available, and the kind of printing and duplicating work the company needs to have done. Take all these factors into consideration as you begin investigating the technical developments that have been made in the field and what new products are on the market.

2 Inspect the equipment that the company currently uses. Is it versatile enough to perform the functions that are required now and those that will be needed in the future? How reliable is it? Does any of it need repair? What are the maintenance costs? How much space does it take up? How difficult is it to operate? How many working hours are spent in producing, collating, and distributing printed material? Would new equipment be cost-efficient, and would it improve the quality of work?

3 Find out what level of understanding the members of the committee already have and how much they need to know. It is necessary for them to have a clear comprehension of cost and quality, but they do not need to become experts in the operation of the equipment.

4 Put together a set of visual aids that will enhance the impact of your presentation. For this particular topic you will have to let the audience see for themselves the difference that new equipment could make. If there is going to be an additional cost in order to obtain better quality, the members of the committee will have to weigh those factors. They will not be able to do that on the basis of your verbal description alone.

5 Have your cost analysis available in printed form. You can display the figures on a flip-chart or overhead projector, or you can give each person a handout sheet. The members of the committee may need to have time to think about what you tell them, and quantitative information is difficult to retain if it is presented only by the spoken word.

6 Be prepared to answer questions. Review what was said in an earlier chapter about how to respond to an audience; the most important thing is to anticipate as best you can what questions might be asked.

THE SALES PRESENTATION

If you are a sales representative, your presentation will be a persuasive talk rather than one that is designed simply to inform. The focus of your talk in this case would be on the value of your product over that which your competitors offer. For example, you might have the opportunity to speak to a budget committee on the advantages of installing a new telephone communication system. In preparing for such a talk you would use all of the same questions of analysis that were just described for developing the informative presentation, and you would try to think of features that your product can offer which the competition does not have. To make a sales presentation, successful companies send out only their very best representatives, because they know that the individual integrity which a presenter is able to convey might be the factor that causes a customer to choose one product over another. Certainly this is true when two sales items are virtually the same.

Customer Service

The fact that commercial products are so frequently similar means that customers often place a high value on service. When selling something as complex as a telephone communication system, a company must be willing to do a great deal more than simply install the equipment and attach written instructions. A very important part of a service contract often includes an instructional program provided by the seller to help users become familiar with all the features of the product. A large organization may have hundreds or even thousands of employees who will be using a phone system, and many of them may not have a strong aptitude for operating technical equipment. Here again is where public speaking and teaching skills can be valuable assets for you to have. To follow up the sale of a communication system, a telephone company will need to send representatives out to the workplaces of the customer to schedule and conduct a series of classes for office personnel in the use of the newly installed equipment. A teaching seminar of this kind should be planned and executed with the same consideration for professionalism as the sales presentation. Again, you will be working with highly paid people who may resent interruptions to their routine and believe that they have more important things to do than listen to a lecture on how to use their telephone. The best seminars of this kind are those that provide operating units for each participant and allow actual hands-on experience in practicing the function after the instructor has explained it. One member of the class can call another, put the person on hold, transfer the call, switch to a speakerphone, initiate a conference call, record a greeting for an answering system, or access a message. All of this can be described rhetorically, but the impact is much greater when the audience becomes actively involved.

Short seminars may work quite well when the subject matter is fairly specific and when there is only a limited need for interaction among the participants, but for an instructional program that is designed to bring about behavioral changes in the ways that people relate to one another in business or personal life, a more intensive approach is required. Such an occasion is often called a *workshop.*

CONDUCTING A WORKSHOP

Workshops of various lengths are commonly sponsored by commercial organizations, government agencies, religious and educational institutions, service clubs, and just about any group that identifies a need for a crash course in skill building. Workshops might be held to teach such subjects as interpersonal communication, leadership, conflict resolution, business management, or self-actualization. They deserve mention here because they are related to the skills we have been discussing in this text.

Conducting a workshop is a communication experience that is challenging and more demanding than simply addressing an audience in a public speaking mode. The workshop leader needs to have considerable depth in understanding the material being presented because there is an opportunity to cover more detail and respond to questions of a rather specific nature. A workshop is generally longer than the average speech, often lasting a full day or several days. The leader will not be lecturing that entire time, of course; there will be demonstrations, small group discussions, and exercises in which the members participate. But the leader needs to structure the entire event so that everything that happens can be related to the central purpose. As a workshop leader you will find yourself becoming closer to your audience than you generally do in a public speaking situation. You may get to know them all by name and gain some understanding of their concerns and levels of comprehension. By the same token they get to know who you are and may come to relate to you in a more familiar fashion. The challenge of being a workshop leader is that you are often seen as a model of what you are teaching, and your ability to demonstrate what you are explaining plays an important part in your overall effectiveness.

Conducting a workshop requires even more planning than goes into a speech. You have a longer period of time to hold the attention of your audience, you need to have a variety of activities so that the participants do not get bored, and you have to keep in mind the sequence of events so ideas unfold in a logical progression. All the while that you are maintaining the structure of the workshop in your mind, you are also using your communication skills to involve the participants by listening to the contributions they make and helping them draw the conclusions you want them to reach. You need to be clear when you tell them how to arrange themselves into small groups, what discussion questions to consider, and when it's time to move on to the next activity. After each event you must be able to regain their attention and get feedback from them as to what transpired in the breakout groups. At the end of the workshop, you have to provide some kind of summary in order to recap what they have learned.

The best workshop leaders generally have a high energy level and a strong commitment to what they are teaching. Tom Peters, coauthor of the book *In Search of Excellence,* is a person frequently called on to conduct workshops on business management. He says, "An audience's biggest turn-on is the speaker's obvious enthusiasm. That's as true for a pitch to purchase a $200,000 computer system as it is for a plea to save the environment. If you're lukewarm about the issue, forget it."[2]

FORMATS FOR SPEAKING OCCASIONS

It's quite possible that a role you might play to facilitate communication is that of the organizer of the function. In this capacity your awareness of the

---

[2] Tom Peters, "On Excellence," *San Jose Mercury News,* July 22, 1991.

needs of a public speaker will help you a great deal, because your job will be to see that the logistical arrangements of the occasion provide the best possible opportunity for participants to speak, to listen, and to comprehend. To help you understand what choices you have, let's look at several different speaking formats.

Interview

A two-person interview is the simplest and most basic unit of interpersonal communication. It can be private, of course, but when we add an audience to the model, we have a format for public address. There are several reasons why it is valuable for us to examine the dynamics of an interview: It is a prominent format for newscasts and public affairs programs on radio and television, and it's an effective way to help knowledgeable people structure their comments when they have had no public speaking training. What you are doing when you interview someone is drawing out the information that interests you (and the audience) without letting the person go off on tangents that are not relevant to the main idea. In other words, the interviewer provides the organizational structure while the person being interviewed relates the information.

You as the Person Interviewed   The interview format is a good place to begin your own public speaking training. Select a topic that is familiar to you. Then, sit down in private with a person who will conduct the interview and work out a set of questions that pertain to the subject matter. The interviewer is going to be one member of your audience, and that person will help you discover what other people want to hear about your topic. You, of course, will also be able to suggest questions that lead into parts of the subject you think is interesting. When you have your list of questions, arrange them in a logical sequence and think about how you are going to respond to each one. Now you are ready to do the interview in front of a real audience. In its entirety the interview contains all the elements of a conventional speech, but the only responsibility you have is to provide the substance in the body of the presentation; the interviewer will do the introduction and the conclusion.

You as the Interviewer   When you are to be the interviewer for a public presentation, take time before you meet the audience to find out what questions the person to be interviewed wants you to ask. During the interview you can extemporize around your list of questions if he or she is reasonably experienced, but it is discourteous to ask something that is going to cause the person embarrassment. The interview format is designed to allow people an opportunity to make the best case they can for the idea they want to express. Your job is to help them do that. Don't turn the interview into a debate, and don't start making a speech of your own.

Symposium

One of the more structured formats is an arrangement called a *symposium*. In setting up a speaking occasion of this kind you would first decide on a topic—one that is clearly stated but fairly broad. For example, you might consider "Alternative Energy Sources in a Petroleum-Based Society." A topic such as this gives speakers a general direction but enough latitude to pursue their own interests. Usually a symposium consists of five or six people who prepare their remarks independently of one another and speak in turn on a given topic for a specific length of time. The topic may be of an informative nature or it could be controversial, and the participants may or may not agree with one another's point of view. "The symposium is suited to programs presented from a stage to a relatively large audience in an auditorium. It is also useful when the occasion calls for more formality and for greater emphasis on the authoritative nature of the participants than can be furnished by a variation of the panel discussion."[3] After all speakers have made their presentations, they would probably respond to questions from the audience or perhaps interact in a less formally structured exchange of ideas. The symposium is not competitive; it is designed to offer information and perhaps arguments that members of an audience can consider and evaluate.

Panel Discussion

A typical format frequently used on television is the panel discussion. This arrangement can also accommodate five or six speakers, but it is less structured than the symposium. Generally the panel discussion will have a moderator who will introduce the topic and pose questions to the panelists. There is no set order in which the participants speak and no specified time limit for each one. They react to the questions as they are moved to do so, and they direct their attention to each other as well as to the audience. In many respects the panel discussion is similar to a conversation; the difference is that the panelists know that an audience is listening and that they need to project their voices with enough volume so they can be heard beyond their immediate circle. Panel members may prepare for a discussion and may even bring notes, but they know that they are not going to express all their comments from start to finish without interruption.

[3] Ernest G. Bormann, *Discussion and Group Methods: Theory and Practice, 2d ed.,* Harper & Row, New York, 1975, p. 325.

They need to be flexible, to listen to what other panelists say, and to be able to respond in an impromptu fashion. The moderator is responsible for getting the discussion started and providing some closure at the end.

OCCASIONS FOR PERSUASIVE SPEAKING

The most challenging formats for public discourse are those designed to address controversial issues. This is the area of public speaking that has the greatest political significance, and traditionally it has been the focal point of our commitment to free speech in this country. The classic dilemma for a society that codifies the right to express opinions is how to structure opportunities for people to say what they want to say without infringing on the rights of others who also want to be heard. For example, we don't want to place restrictions on our senators and representatives in Congress, so we allow them unlimited debate. But when one legislator gets the floor, he or she is free to filibuster so that no one else has a chance to speak. Is that a strategy that contributes to free expression, or does it have the opposite effect?

Let's look at another example. In 1969 the president of San Francisco State College, S. I. Hayakawa (a noted semanticist and, later, a U.S. senator), was trying to speak on the campus when his words were drowned out by a sound truck that was being used by a group of student protesters. Hayakawa attempted several times to make himself heard over the more powerful amplification of the sound system. Finally, he leaped up onto the truck and pulled the wires out of the speakers. It was a dramatic incident, praised by some and condemned by others. You be the judge: Whose rights were violated?

Freedom of speech cannot exist in a social structure that has no restraints; yet, if we have rules of conduct that are too rigid, we stifle creative expression. The formats we provide for public discourse need to have a reasonable amount of flexibility, but sufficient structure to see that all parties are treated fairly.

Town Meetings

Ever since the colonists first came to America, there has been a tradition in this country of holding town meetings. Generally the topics are of a local nature, but they could deal with just about any social issue. The town meeting format is often used when a city council gathers to address a controversial issue and allows members of the community to present their views. The agenda item might be to grant a building permit for a shopping mall or to ban the sale of alcoholic beverages; whatever it is, all interested parties can have their say. The problem is that when a lot of people want to speak, there isn't enough time for everyone to be heard; so some restrictions are necessary. If you are handling the arrangements for a public forum, there are several tactics you can use to see that the proceedings are fair and orderly. One is to have the people who want to speak list their names beforehand. Another way is to place two microphones on opposite sides of the hall and let people line up behind either one. A moderator can then call up each speaker, alternating from one line to the other. In order to accommodate as many people as possible you would have to set a time limit—perhaps 3 to 5 minutes—and be sure that it is enforced.

If you are a speaker at such a meeting, your challenge will be to say as much as you can, and advance your strongest arguments in the least possible time. Often it is much harder to give a short speech than a long one. Every word and phrase has to have impact. Try to eliminate delays in your speech pattern, and avoid taking up time with verbal pauses such as, "uh, let me see."

When you participate in a town meeting discussion, remember who the decision makers are. Your goal here is a little different than it is in the normal public speaking situation. What you say doesn't have to please the whole audience; the people you want to convince are the members of the city council. There may be only seven of them, and all you have to do is win four of their votes. Your audience-analysis skills are very important in this kind of situation. Learn as much as you can about the individual characteristics and the inclinations of those who are going to cast votes. Give special consideration to the ones who might be undecided about the issue. You might even refer to them by name in order to get their attention, and speak to them in a way that appeals to their reason. Don't make accusations; that has a negative effect. And don't bother trying to convince members of the council whom you know to be strongly opposed. You don't need their votes if you have four who are on your side.

Debate

We hear the word *debate* used in a great many ways. A conversation can become a debate if two people identify that they have conflicting viewpoints on a particular issue. During election campaigns there are often occasions on radio and television when the candidates will hold a debate. In order to have a clear picture of what we really mean by the word, we have to establish what the *format* is going to be. The presidential debates we have seen and heard in recent years have consisted of newspeople asking the candidates a series of questions in a subject area that is often extremely broad. One debate might be on "international affairs" and another on "domestic issues." The candidates have a specified amount of time to respond to the questions, after which there may be a rebuttal pe-

Learning the skills of debate will help you if you run for office.

riod. Frequently these media events degenerate into a barrage of accusations and campaign rhetoric that sheds very little light on the real differences in policies. Seldom is there time for any of the candidates to do a thorough analysis of an issue or pursue a line of argumentation in depth. Campaign strategists seem to believe that the American public has a limited tolerance for intelligent discussions of social concerns.

Traditionally, debate is associated with the word *forensics*—the Greek word for "argumentative speaking." The philosopher Protagoras (481–411 B.C.) taught his students to reason by requiring that they be able to debate both sides of a controversial issue. This practice seems as though it would force students to compromise their ethical standards by having them express ideas that they did not truly believe. But we need to understand that forensic activities were regarded then, as they are now, to be academic exercises in rhetorical analysis. If an issue is truly controversial, there are going to be arguments to support more than one side. The challenge to the student is to discover what those arguments are, examine them for validity, and advance them to see how well they can be established. If students are unable to understand the arguments of the opposition, they are not fully informed on the issue and their own reasoning may be flawed. In today's college debate tournaments we follow the same practice. A team is required to debate the affirmative side of the issue in one round and take the negative side in the next. The result is that debaters are ultimately able to base their opinions on reasons that can stand the test of refutation.

As a college student interested in speech activities, you might become part of a forensics program and participate as a debater. When you do that, you will study the theory and practice of argumentation in considerable depth and will learn strategies that are applicable in the courtroom as well as on the speaker's podium. For now, we need to look only at the basic format so that if the opportunity arose, you would be able to make arrangements for holding a debate.

Phrasing the Question   A debate proposition is called a *question,* and it is always phrased so that it challenges the status quo. The rationale behind this is that if there were no objections to the status quo, there would be no reason for a debate. A question of policy pertaining to U.S. relations with Central America might be phrased as follows:

Resolved: That capital punishment should be abolished in the United States.

Note that the proposition is stated as though it were being phrased by the *affirmative* side. These team members are the ones who have to demonstrate that there is a reason for the debate; therefore, they have the opportunity to speak first.

The Affirmative's Responsibilities   A basic principle of the United States justice system is that a person is innocent until proved guilty. For this reason, the prosecution has what we call the *burden of proof.* Debaters on the affirmative side have the same responsibility. They must show that there is a need for a change in the status quo or that there are inherent disadvantages to existing policy. They must also demonstrate that the plan they offer would correct the needs they have described or that significant benefits would result from the changes they recommend.

The Negative's Responsibilities   The debaters on the negative side can take one of three approaches: (1) They can give *straight refutation,* showing that the status quo is perfectly adequate and that the affirmative's plan is unnecessary, unworkable, or disadvantageous. (2) They can present a *repairs case,* in which they acknowledge that while the existing policy may be flawed, the problems are minor ones and can be corrected without making inherent changes in the status quo. (3) They can present a *counterplan,* in which they admit that there is a need for a change but offer a policy that is significantly different from that which the affirmative recommends. This third approach is a risky one for the negative because they are forced to agree with a great deal of the affirmative's analysis. Furthermore, they take on the same burden of proof that had been the affirmative's responsibility. The negative debaters must be able to convince a judge that their plan is inherently different from that of the affirmative and is significantly superior.

Sequence of Speeches   The sequence in which the debaters speak will depend on the number of people in the contest, the time limitations, the extent of audience or panel participation, and the general format of the debate. The structure that is often used in competitive college debate is the standard Oxford style, which calls for a very specific sequence. Normally there are two debaters on each side speaking alternately, with the first affirmative beginning the round.

First affirmative	10 minutes
First negative	10 minutes
Second affirmative	10 minutes
Second negative	10 minutes

Each of the four people has the same amount of time to lay out a case, which is called a *constructive* speech. All the main contentions that the debaters intend to put forth must be included in this first part of the debate; no new issues may be introduced in rebuttal. The second part of the debate is called the *rebuttal period.* At this time the debaters attack the arguments that have been raised against them and attempt to reestablish their own cases. The rebuttals begin with the first negative speaker and end with the second affirmative as follows:

First negative	5 minutes
First affirmative	5 minutes
Second negative	5 minutes
Second affirmative	5 minutes

Because the affirmative debaters have the burden of proof, they are given the opportunity to begin and end the debate. The affirmative must present a *prima facie case*—one that has no inherent weaknesses. It must be able to stand on its own merits unless one or more of its main contentions are discredited. In other words, the plan must either solve the problems of the status quo or demonstrate significant advantages. The negative must clash with the structural arguments of the affirmative and, to win the debate, must successfully refute one or more of the opposition's main contentions.

Variations   There are several possible variations on the basic structure of a debate round. One that is quite common is a *cross-examination* period during the constructive speeches when debaters have the opportunity to ask questions of the opposition. Another variation is to cast the proposition in the form of a question of fact or a question of value. For example, the Central America issue might be phrased in one of the following ways:

(Question of fact) Resolved: That the death penalty is a deterrent to capital crime.

(Question of value) Resolved: That the death penalty violates the moral integrity of the nation.

When the proposition is one that involves a question of fact or a question of value, the debate takes on a different tone than it does for a question of policy. The information gathered for a question of fact would be of a historical nature, and for a question of value it would be more philosophical. There would be no requirement for a prima facie case on the part of the affirmative and no need for a plan of action. Argumentation and refutation would stand on their own merits rather than being measured against criteria for specific responsibilities.

Judging   A major difficulty that plagues organizers of debate tournaments is finding qualified judges. Academically one might argue that a debate tournament is simply a means of stimulating thought and teaching skills of critical thinking. Realistically, however, students are motivated by competitive energy, and they want to be rewarded if they win. Preparing for a debate is one of the most rigorous intellectual challenges students can accept, and they have a right to be evaluated by competent and impartial judges. If they are not, they will learn a lesson that none of us wants to teach: That the rules of society are determined by people in authority whose minds are already made up and who don't respond to rational arguments.

THE HUNDREDTH MONKEY

Sometimes you may feel as though there is nothing you can say that will have any effect on what people do or what they believe. If you have a concern for social issues, you may get discouraged when you read about government policies that seem to ignore human needs, business ventures that perpetuate greed and corruption, or industrial practices that pollute the environment. But before you become resigned to accept what appears to be the inevitable, consider the notion that has been advanced by Ken Keyes, Jr., in a book called *The Hundredth Monkey*. He describes a study made of a species of Japanese monkey that had been observed in the wild on the island of Koshima for a period of 30 years. The study began in 1952 when scientists began dropping sweet potatoes into the sand on the island to add to the monkeys' diet. The monkeys liked the potato, but didn't like the taste of the dirt on them. One monkey solved the problem by learning to wash the potato in a stream. This practice was picked up by a few other monkeys, but after several years the scientists observed that there were still a great many monkeys who had not learned the trick. Keyes relates:

> Then something took place. In the autumn of 1958, a certain number of Koshima monkeys were washing sweet potatoes—the exact number is not known. Let us suppose that when the sun rose one morning, there were 99 monkeys on Koshima Island who had learned to wash their sweet potatoes. Let's further assume that later that morning the hundredth monkey learned to wash sweet potatoes. Then it happened. By that evening almost everyone in the tribe was washing sweet potatoes before eating them. That added energy of this hundredth monkey somehow created an ideological breakthrough.[4]

You never know when you might be the person to influence the "hundredth monkey" by saying the right thing at the right time. If there is validity to the theory that Ken Keyes advances, and if it applies to human behavior, your efforts to make constructive social changes by talking to people can make a difference.

EXERCISE

Begin this exercise by getting together in a group of four people to practice debate. Two of you are going to support the affirmative side of the issue; the other two will support the negative. Remember that this is a rhetorical exercise, so the side you are assigned to defend may or may not be the one that you actually favor. To simplify the research, set a time when all four of you can go to the library together. Look through a stack of periodicals called *Congressional Digest* and decide on the subject for your debate. The topics are clearly indicated on the cover of each magazine, and inside you will find arguments for (pro) and against (con). After that, phrase the debate topic so you all know which side you are defending; you can write it in the form of a question of policy, a question of fact, or a question of value. Go to other sources for more information, but you will find a good deal of what you need in that one magazine. Each of you will give the first constructive speech as prescribed for Oxford-style debate. Remember that the affirmative has the burden of proof, so the debate starts with a speaker from that side.

---

[4] Ken Keyes, Jr., *The Hundredth Monkey,* Vision Books, Coos Bay, Ore., 1982, pp. 11–15.

QUESTIONS FOR REVIEW

1 What kinds of things should be said when you are giving a toast?

2 What is the main purpose of expressing thanks to people publicly?

3 What information should be included when you are making a notable achievement award?

4 What is meant by using the methodology of the journalist when you are announcing a coming event? What details should be included in such an announcement?

5 What guidelines would you set for giving a speech introduction?

6 In order to make your informative presentation effective, how can you reinforce retention of your quantitative information?

7 What should be the focus of your talk when you are making a sales presentation? What might you want to emphasize if your product is similar in cost and quality to that of the competition?

8 What kind of speaking occasion might follow the sale of a complex product such as a phone system or computer program?

9 Why do newspeople on radio and television often use the interview format rather than simply having a knowledgeable person give a speech? How can being interviewed help you become a better public speaker?

10 What is a symposium and how does it differ from a panel discussion?

11 How can you structure a town meeting format so that everyone who wants to speak has a chance to be heard?

12 What is the advantage of having students debate first one side of a controversial issue and then the other?

13 What are the responsibilities of the affirmative debaters?

14 What are three strategies that can be used by negative debaters?

15 Who speaks first in a debate? What is meant by the *burden of proof?*

CHAPTER 11

MEETING ETHICAL STANDARDS

Any criteria for evaluation in public address must include the ethical qualities of the speaker. The reference here is to the mode of proof that Aristotle calls the *ethos*. The very essence of persuasion has its roots in the ethos because the other two modes of proof, the logos and the pathos, will fail to persuade unless the audience perceives the speaker to be a person of good character. When the integrity of the speaker is in doubt, listeners will question the validity of the evidence and will resist being moved by any attempted emotional appeal.

Whenever speakers step on to a podium, they must remember that the ethical qualities they project are going to be evaluated by the audience. This is an important consideration for every speaker, but particularly for those who are in positions of public trust. Frequently we pick up a newspaper and see headlines referring to an investigation conducted by the Senate or the House Ethics Committee into the affairs of a senator or congressional representative. Generally the investigation is prompted by a suspicion that the party in question has been in violation of a law such as misuse of campaign funds or accepting of gratuities for favors. Certainly legal restrictions can be used as one means of measuring ethical standards, but for purposes of rhetorical analysis we need to examine what speakers *say* as well as what they *do*.

ETHICAL STANDARDS FOR PUBLIC SPEAKERS

The Roman philosopher Quintilian (A.D. 40–118) regarded the speaker's moral integrity as an essential element in rhetorical evaluation. A speech of lofty purpose, he maintained, must be delivered by a "good man speaking well." Setting aside the obvious sexism of his claim, we note that the character of the speaker in the classical view is inextricably tied to the quality of the speech itself. The same observation was made four centuries earlier by Aristotle:

> There are three reasons why speakers themselves are persuasive; these are *practical wisdom* and *virtue* and *goodwill*. . . . Speakers make mistakes in what they say or advise through failure to exhibit either all or one of these; for either through lack of practical sense they do not form opinions rightly; or though forming opinions rightly they do not say what they think because of a bad character; or they are prudent and fair-minded but lack goodwill; so that it is possible for people not to give the best advice although they know what it is.[1]

Let's look more closely at Aristotle's three criteria: (1) Practical wisdom or sense means that the speaker is knowledgeable and is able to reason clearly, to consider supporting evidence, and to use good judgment in arriving at conclusions. (2) Virtue means that the speaker will not knowingly lie to the audience or withhold information that is necessary for listeners to understand what they need to know. (3) Goodwill means that what the speaker is advocating is in the best interest of the audience.

The Ethic of Good Sense

If speakers were forced to comply with Aristotle's criteria, the first one alone—having practical sense—would probably keep a great many of them off the podium altogether. But who is to make that determination? There will always be those who believe that even the most poorly reasoned speech is to be applauded. Just about anyone who has the mental capacity to utter sounds from behind a lectern will receive a measure of support from someone. All we can say is that practical sense can be judged only by "sensible critics"—those in the audience who are listening with a critical ear and are able to perceive whether or not the message of the speaker conforms to sensible standards. If the speaker succeeds in reaching only the uncritical members of the audience—those who are willing to accept platitudes and unsupported assertions—we would say that the speech has failed to inspire confidence in the orator's character.

[1] *Aristotle, On Rhetoric,* George A. Kennedy (trans.), Oxford University Press, New York, 1991, pp. 120–121.

Speakers who fail to meet the criterion of having practical sense might have a temporary measure of success, but they can very quickly fall from grace when the audience catches on to what they are doing. One such speaker was Senator Joseph McCarthy, who enjoyed considerable praise from his supporters for many years as he carried on his campaign to weed communists out of government. He was finally stopped by a resolution of censure when a majority of senators recognized that he was making irresponsible charges against innocent people without having evidence for his accusations.

The Ethic of Good Moral Character

Using the federal government as a model we can find a number of cases to use as examples of moral character. During the Iran-Contra investigation in 1986 Colonel Oliver North was called upon to testify regarding his role in the affair. He openly acknowledged that on a previous occasion he had lied to Congress about a deal to sell arms to Iran and use the money to aid the Contra rebels fighting in Nicaragua. Clearly this is a violation of Aristotle's criterion of not making false statements, but is a person's integrity restored after admitting the lie? How should he be judged on a balance of both occasions? And there is yet another question: Colonel North claimed that he lied because he believed it was in the best interest of the country to do so. Can a lie told by a speaker ever be justified? If the public had considered his cause to have had merit, should he have been exonerated?

In regard to Ronald Reagan's role in the Iran-Contra affair, there are other vital questions: Did the President know about the deal? And if so, when did he know it? Did he lie to the press when he said that no arms were being sold to Iran? Again in this case we can see how Aristotle's criteria can be applied. If President Reagan knew of the transaction, he would have been guilty of making a false statement. If he did not know, he would be in violation of the "good sense" criterion, because a president should certainly have knowledge of the activities of his own staff.

The Ethic of Goodwill

Charges brought against Alan Cranston by the Senate Ethics Committee illustrate another of Aristotle's criteria. An accusation was made by the committee that Senator Cranston had accepted campaign contributions in exchange for supporting legislative decisions that were in the favor of banking investor Charles Keating. When asked by the press if he thought that his campaign contributions in any way influenced Senator Cranston's vote, Mr. Keating replied, "I certainly hope so." The question here is one that addresses Aristotle's third criterion—being disposed to the goodwill of the audience. When the senator spoke on behalf of legislative decisions that favored Mr. Keating, did he have the welfare of his constituents in mind, or was he thinking primarily of his own interests? In studying rhetorical ethics it is necessary for us to consider the *motives* of the speaker as well as the verbal expression.

POLITICAL ETHICS

It would almost seem as though the term *political ethics* is an oxymoron. Is it possible for anyone to hold an elected position and still be able to maintain high ethical standards? Politicians sometimes refer to the "rule of survival," which means that they have to save their seats before they can save the world. There are many intelligent, highly qualified people in this country who would make excellent legislators but do not run for office because of the compromises they believe they would have to make in their principles in order to get elected. Members of the United States House of Representatives must run for office every two years; that means a person in Congress needs to be campaigning almost all the time. Political campaigns cost a great deal of money, and politicians need to gain the favor of large contributors in order to build up what they call their "war chests." This certainly does not justify making exaggerated promises or accepting fees for favors, but it helps us to understand the pressure that is placed on a person who makes politics a career.

One former U.S. representative, Paul "Pete" McCloskey from California, who served for twenty years in Congress, speaks frequently on the subject of ethics in politics. His advice to young people who are considering running for office is to wait until they have established their careers in the private sector before they subject themselves to the rigors of an elected position. By doing this, he says, you do not become dependent on the political office for your livelihood; you are free to say "no" to those who try to buy your vote. Then, if you lose an election, you have a career to fall back on.

The pressure on a politician to get reelected can be illustrated in the example of Richard Nixon's involvement in the Watergate scandal. Overzealous supporters of the Republican party hired burglars to break into Democratic headquarters to learn about political strategies of the opposition. It was a clumsy and unnecessary act because the polls showed Nixon leading his opponent, George McGovern, by a comfortable margin. The discovery that the President and his advisers had authorized the break-in had devastating consequences. Political writers frequently compare this issue with the Iran-Contra affair and observe that the violation which occurred in Ronald Reagan's administration was far more serious than the one that led to the resignation of Richard Nixon. Why is it that Congress

Politicians are under preasure to hold their seat in office but still make ethical choices.

and the general public were as upset as they were over the relatively mild infraction that was committed by the staff of Richard Nixon? It's true that the President lied about his involvement in the matter, but no serious harm was done either to the nation or to the Democratic party, so why the big fuss? It is apparent that in the eyes of the American public the *act* of lying is a more serious ethical violation than the subject about which the lie is told. Another observation we might make is that a lie is worse when it is told by a person who is in a high position of public trust.

THE ETHICS OF SOUND REASONING

The philosophers in ancient Greece had a term for the disregard of the principles of logic, reasoning, good sense, and sound ethical practices. The word was *sophistry*. Originally it applied to a person of great wisdom—a teacher of rhetoric—but as those who taught the art began to instruct their students in ways to deceive the audience and to make, as Socrates said, the "worse appear to be the better reason," the reputation of the sophists became severely tarnished. Today the word is used in an accusatory fashion in reference to someone who attempts to manipulate an audience into accepting specious reasoning.

Unfortunately, such manipulation is frequently successful. When the audience is not diligent, speakers are able to base their claims on flimsy ethical standards without being challenged. What this observation suggests is that a speaker's moral integrity needs to be no higher than that of the audience being addressed. When this condition prevails, false notions are perpetuated and gradually emerge as popular "truths."

ETHICAL FALLACIES

It has been said that human beings are not so much rational animals as they are *rationalizing* animals. We tend to invent reasons why we should go on believing what we want to believe, even though there is no logical or moral justification for the belief. If these rationalizations are not recognized for what they are, they begin to take on the appearance of having validity when actually they are manipulative devices that we could call *ethical fallacies*.

Caveat Emptor

This is a Latin phrase that means "Let the buyer beware." Merchants have retreated to this rationale for as long as there have been commercial transactions. The fallacy claims that it is the responsibility of the receiver, not the presenter, to discover flaws in the merchandise. In the context of public speaking, it suggests that if the audience is foolish enough to accept a spurious argument, they deserve what they get.

Everyone Is Doing It

This is one of the favorite ploys of teenagers who want to get parents to believe that a particular behavior is perfectly acceptable. The term *everyone* is generally a hyperbole and may include only a few close friends. But it's also important to recognize the fallacy that conformity is not necessarily a valid criterion for acceptable behavior.

The Only Crime Is Getting Caught

This fallacy says that if you are smart, you deserve to get away with anything you want to do. It suggests that self-interest is the only moral imperative and that there is no intrinsic value in doing the right thing. It is, of course, a blatant violation of any ethical standard, but is all too frequently used as a basis for behavior.

If I Didn't Do It, Someone Else Would

This claim might be made by someone to justify their being engaged in an illegal or immoral activity, such as selling narcotics or taking bribes. It could never be a defensible position for any responsible speaker because it ignores the fact that if nobody did it, the deed would not be done.

You Can Steal from the Rich Because They Can Afford It

Many people erroneously believe that nobody gets hurt when a big company is the victim. In reality, however, industry loses billions of dollars every year from the theft of tools and office supplies. Insurance companies are frequently targets of this fallacious reasoning when people who are otherwise fair and law-abiding citizens see nothing wrong with filing exaggerated claims for losses and suing for amounts far in excess of their pain and suffering. Unfortunately, the more people do this, the more it seems to be acceptable, and the result is higher consumer costs for everyone.

It Doesn't Matter Because Nothing Will Change Anyway

This moral fallacy allows people to avoid their responsibilities out of a feeling of futility and fatalism. It is a reason given by those who don't vote in elections and who pay no attention to current events. When this becomes a pervasive point of view in a democratic society, the groundwork is laid for abusive corruption and the erosion of human rights.

MORAL INTEGRITY

Maintaining a high ethical standard is not something you can turn on when you step onto the podium and turn off when you step down. It is a quality that must be consistent in the personality and character of anyone who intends to engage in public address. Whenever you face an audience, you reveal not only your point of view but also your moral integrity. If there are flaws in your character that you are trying to hide, your public speaking experiences will begin to feel uncomfortable.

We cannot legislate against ethical fallacies—and certainly we would not want to do so. Any moral standards that we establish must be founded on principles of reason and accepted on their own merit, rather than being prescribed by law. As an individual, you may have your own code of ethics that perhaps is working well for you. But as you begin to extend yourself to others, as you do when you speak in public, you may need to expand upon your code so that it includes a broader range of situations and takes into consideration your community responsibilities. Fortunately, we do not have to embark upon that task alone and unassisted; there is a great deal of philosophical groundwork that has already been laid.

UTILITARIAN ETHICS

The philosophy of utilitarian ethics has a great deal of appeal because it is flexible and permits adjustment on the basis of changing social mores. It states that actions should be judged in terms of the good that results, compared with the harm that is done. If there is more benefit than there is maleficence, the action should be regarded as ethical. This philosophy was espoused by John Stuart Mill, who published his thesis *Utilitarianism* in 1861. He maintained that pleasure or happiness is a basic good and there is no reason why it should not be pursued by everyone. We need to add a qualification, however, because such a thesis, standing alone, seems to give license to putting personal interest above any other value:

> . . . if each of us recognizes that our own happiness is intrinsically valuable, Mill seems to conclude, then each of us must also recognize that everyone else's happiness has a similar value. . . . And so, Mill claims, we all ought to pursue the general happiness, that is, the happiness of everyone, including ourselves.[2]

---

[2] Manuel Velasquez and Cynthia Rostankowski, *Ethics: Theory and Practice,* Prentice-Hall, Englewood Cliffs, N.J., 1985, p. 107.

When we step into the speaker's platform, we are extending our values to others.

The idea seems to be similar to that which Thomas Jefferson expressed in the Declaration of Independence: "We hold these truths to be self evident, that all men are created equal, that they are endowed by their Creator with certain unalienable Rights, that among these are Life, Liberty, and the pursuit of Happiness."

Both Mill and Jefferson started with the premise that happiness is intrinsically good and that there is no virtue in preventing others or yourself from having it. Jefferson took the principle a step farther and made it part of a social system. Furthermore, he sealed it in concrete by saying that the right was "endowed by the creator." It's hard to argue with a mandate like that! The problem with Mill's philosophy is that it assumes that whatever brings happiness to you will also bring happiness to others.

A Contemporary Version of Utilitarian Ethics

In order for a social climate to exist that will permit people to exercise their right to pursue happiness, there must be rules, some of which will have the force of law. We would like to think that the rules and laws of our society are set in place to allow us maximum opportunity to pursue happiness, but we know that is not always the case.

Richard Brandt has offered a contemporary theory that he calls "rule utilitarianism." His premise is that we should act only according to those rules which we think will promote the greatest happiness. This implies that we are not morally obligated to obey *any* injunction that is called a "rule" but only the ones which are in the best interest of those who are affected by the rule. Brandt explains:

> It would make concessions to the fact that ordinary people are not capable of perfectly fine discriminations, and to the fact that, not being morally perfect, people of ordinary conscientiousness will have a tendency to abuse a moral rule where it suits their interests. We must remember that a college dormitory rule like "Don't play music at such times or in such a way as to disturb the study or sleep of others" would be ideally flexible if people were perfect; since they aren't, we have to settle for a rule like "No music after 10 p.m."[3]

As reasonable people, we have no problem recognizing the need for such a rule because we know that it benefits most of the people most of the time and imposes minimum inconvenience upon those who are restricted by it.

---

[3] Richard B. Brandt, "Toward a Credible Form of Utilitarianism," *Morality and the Language of Conduct,* Wayne State University Press, Detroit, 1963, p. 124.

THE ETHICS OF CIVIL DISOBEDIENCE

What if a rule or law is not reasonable? Can a speaker ethically advocate the breaking of a rule in a society that is committed to creating an environment which makes the pursuit of happiness a God-given right? The qualification that Brandt provides in rule utilitarianism recognizes the need for structure within a society but allows for protest against unjust laws. In his essay "Civil Disobedience," Henry David Thoreau wrote, "If the law is of such a nature that it requires you to be an agent of injustice to another, then I say, break the law. Let your life be a counter friction to stop the machine."

The consideration that civil disobedience could be included in the ethical criteria for public speakers is certain to draw objection from those who subscribe to law and order. Yet, the issue must be raised because of the integrity and prestige of the people who espoused their right to protest legal statutes that violated their personal moral code. The fact that Martin Luther King is a national hero and is honored with a day that commemorates his birth is testimony to the ethical status of nonviolent protest.

Civil disobedience does not mean that you have a right to break any law you don't like without paying a price. Thoreau, King, and others who were principal players in civil protests took the action they did with full knowledge of the consequences and with the willingness to accept the penalties of the law. Furthermore, they were prepared to defend their actions in open forum with reason and evidence.

When the civil rights movement is measured by the standards of utilitarian ethics, we see that the benefits did finally come to outweigh the disruption of the society. The fact that the laws which restricted racial equality were eventually struck down vindicated those who brought about the change through their physical and rhetorical protests.

Utilitarian ethics works well as a means of finding justification for our own interests, but it can blind us to the hardships of others. It relies heavily on contemporary cultural mores and often permits social injustices. In the years before the Civil War, advocates of slavery were able to maintain their position because in their local regions they had popular support. They could argue that a greater good was being served since slaves on the southern plantations were helping to assure economic stability and provide prosperity for the whole population. Furthermore, they could assert that slaves in the south were generally treated better than the free workers in the northern factories. The reasoning of those who are guided by the code of utilitarianism is that there can be no universally accepted standard for moral behavior.

CATEGORICAL IMPERATIVES

In the eighteenth century Immanuel Kant argued in support of what he called *categorical imperatives*—principles that are constant and not affected by changing social circumstances. We see this philosophy applied in some elements of our culture today. In the traditional family, parents may attempt to instill values in their children, teaching them to be honest and self-reliant regardless of the behavior of their peers. The Boy Scout and Girl Scout Law has served a valuable purpose for many generations, teaching young people to be trustworthy, loyal, helpful, friendly, courteous, kind, obedient, cheerful, thrifty, brave, clean, and reverent. While it may seem as though there are no categorical imperatives, when we examine the moral codes of social and religious institutions, we see that there are a great many similar principles to which people of goodwill in almost all cultures could probably agree.

Kant believed that abiding by categorical imperatives would be mutually beneficial to all of humankind, and that we should live our lives as though we were models for everyone else to follow. He said, "I am never to act unless I am acting on a maxim that I *will* to become universal law." The philosophy expressed here is that when you abuse a universal principle which protects human rights and dignity, you are doing harm to yourself as well as to those whom you have offended. Another writer who expressed the same thought was the Roman philosopher Terence who said, "Nothing of mankind is alien unto me." The English poet John Donne observed that "No man is an island" and that each individual has the responsibility to protect the rights of everyone else. "Never send to know for whom the bell tolls," said Donne. "It tolls for thee."

The Kantian philosophy does not have the flexibility of Mill's utilitarianism, because it requires maintaining the constancy of a principle regardless of the consequences. For example, a categorical imperative might be that slavery is wrong. Even though there are economic advantages and perhaps (as southerners argued) benefits to the slaves themselves, the very notion of slavery is a violation of moral principles, and there is no social value that could give it redemption. In reference to this analysis, it is interesting to note that Jefferson used phrases that sounded like categorical imperatives: "All men are created equal . . . [and] are endowed by their Creator with certain unalienable rights." Yet, in 1776 those rights belonged only to white, male property owners, not to women or to slaves. In this respect his edict was utilitarian.

In more recent times we can see what an important difference there is between the utilitarian philosophy and categorical imperatives. On March 16, 1968, American soldiers killed several hundred civilians, many of them women and children, in the town of My Lai in Vietnam. Can such an act have any justification? The utilitarian could argue that while the event was a terrible tragedy, it was necessary given the circumstances of the war: American soldiers never knew when a civilian, even a child, would have a hand grenade concealed and ready to explode. Therefore, our troops did what they needed to do in order to survive.

The Kantian philosophy, on the other hand, would be that the killing of civilians, even in wartime, is a violation of a basic categorical imperative and is not justifiable under any circumstances. This was, in fact, the ruling of a military court that tried and convicted Lieutenant William Calley for the responsibility of commanding and participating in the act.

SOCIAL CONTRACTS

Civilization depends on social contracts. Society cannot allow all people to follow their own interests at the expense of others, so we establish laws, customs, and codes to govern and regulate individual behavior. But on what basis do we make those rules?

Harvard University professor and philosopher John Rawls suggests that idealistically, the rules of a society should be established by reasonable people who are acting in their own self-interest, but who do not know in advance what their position in the society will be. They would not know, for example, if they will be male or female, black or white, young or old, rich or poor. Being reasonable and acting in their own self-interest, they would not pass laws that would discriminate against any particular sex, race, age group, or social class, because such discrimination might ultimately infringe on their own welfare. Rawls says, "The intuitive idea is that since everyone's well-being depends upon a scheme of cooperation without which no one could have a satisfactory life, the division of advantages should be such as to draw forth the willing cooperation of everyone taking part in it."[4]

This perspective may help us to establish a basis for our moral values because, as speakers, we do make contributions to social contracts. It is not enough for us to think in terms limited to our own conduct; we need to look for a philosophy that pertains to *policy*. We know that when we step onto the speaker's platform, we are extending our values to others, and even if we declare that we are speaking for ourselves, we are at the same time modeling what we would prescribe for those we address.

---

[4] John Rawls, *A Theory of Justice,* The Belknap Press of Harvard University Press, Cambridge, Mass., 1971, p. 15.

THE VALUE OF ETHICAL CONDUCT

But what is the real value of ethical conduct? If the audience likes the speech, why should we, as speakers, be concerned about whether or not it conforms to ethical standards? That's an important question for us to address because altruism may not be sufficient motivation for those whose actions are normally governed primarily by self-interest.

1 The practical value. The speaker whose position is based on sound ethical standards will be perceived by an audience as someone who can be believed and trusted. Therefore, the speech has a better chance to succeed.

2 The intrinsic value. This is value for its own sake. It is not measurable in terms of rewards, but it generates confidence and self-esteem within the speaker who can say, "In my heart I know I'm right."

3 The social value. Any society will work better if its people subscribe to and behave according to rules and principles that are just. Those who speak in public have an added responsibility because they influence the thought and behavior of others.

All of this may sound as though demands are being placed on public speakers to be perfect in all respects. Not so. We all make mistakes and fail from time to time to abide by even those moral principles we have established for ourselves. But the fact that we commit indiscretions does not mean that we should advocate them. If a man is unfaithful to his wife, he need not feel that he must stand upon the podium and advocate infidelity. In public speaking, we profess what we believe *should* prevail. If we acknowledge transgressions in our own behavior, it would be only to illustrate the point that there is need for vigilance against future misconduct.

Public speaking differs from other forms of discourse in a very important way. In private conversations or in closed meetings, we can explore problems and perhaps try out ideas by expressing them tentatively without having them become open declarations. But in public address we are standing on what we profess to be our considered and reasoned values and opinions.

THE SPEAKER'S CODE OF ETHICS

Almost every profession has its code of ethics; doctors, lawyers, broadcasters, journalists—all have established standards of ethical conduct. That is not to say that everyone in each of those professions abides by the standards to the letter. There is no force of law that compels them to do so, only their own sense of moral obligation and regard for their professional reputation. Schools, colleges, and universities require that graduates have an understanding of ethical standards in their field of study in order to maintain the historical tradition and the integrity of the profession.

In 1972 the Speech Communication Association adopted a Credo for Free and Responsible Communication in a Democratic Society. It condemns the use of physical and coercive interference with the free speech of others; it urges respect for accuracy in communication and for reasoning based on evidence. While the ability to speak in public is not something that requires a license or a degree, it is a recognized academic discipline, and students who choose to study the art at the college or university level should have the same appreciation for a code of ethics as people who pursue professional careers. Those of us who teach public address certainly have a professional responsibility to see that ethical standards are observed in the classroom. As someone who is beginning to practice the art of public speaking, you will have to work out your own code for yourself. Some conditions that you might think about including are as follows:

1 The claims of the speaker must be based on accurate information, and no false or misleading evidence must be presented to the audience.

2 No information that would have a significant bearing on the speaker's claim must knowingly be withheld from the audience.

3 Recommendations made by the speaker must be in the best interest of the audience, and any personal gain for the speaker must be clearly understood by the audience.

4 The message must clarify what the probable consequences would be and who, if anyone, would be adversely affected if the claims of the speaker were to be accepted.

5 The speaker must be prepared to take responsibility for claims made and be willing to speak in their support if called upon to do so.

6 The information of the speaker must be presented with the intent to clarify the issue rather than obscure or confuse it.

The conditions of this code do not provide any guidance for positions taken on particular issues, nor do they specify what moral principles should be followed. The implementation of the code is the responsibility of the speaker, and the interpretation must be that of the critic. Furthermore, the code is by no means comprehensive; there are a number of significant questions that are left unanswered.

Does the End Justify the Means?

Students of philosophy continue to wrestle with this question. Is it ethical to set aside a moral principle if a greater good is the result of the action? Would you, for example, condone torture as a means of obtaining information from a terrorist in order to save the lives of hostages? If you subscribe to the philosophy of categorical imperatives, you would have to say no. If you apply the principles of utilitarianism, you would need to weigh the harmful consequences against the benefits of the end results.

Is Omission as Bad as Commission?

Certainly, if you lie to an audience, you are violating a basic ethical standard. But what if you are in a position to give needed information and you fail to do so? Is it a breach of ethics for the victim of a crime or misconduct to abstain from pressing charges? Is a woman who has been sexually abused or harassed guilty of an ethical omission if she fails to come forward with information that would identify the offending party? How does such omission compare with a false accusation?

What Is the Best Response to Make to Charges of Misconduct?

Making a public statement to defend yourself against charges of misconduct is probably not something you will be called upon to do unless you are a prominent figure. But what would you do if you were in this position? Would you be open and candid even if it meant jeopardizing the reputation of another party? If a person refuses to answer the charges, is he or she committing an ethical violation. Is honesty always the best policy? We can see from the past experience of high officials in government that attempts to cover up transgressions can sometimes be more damaging to a cause than the mistake itself.

REASON IS THE ULTIMATE ETHIC

In the final analysis reason must be the basis for any ethical code. We strive to do the right thing, not for the sake of demonstrating altruism but because we know that it is ultimately in our own interest and that of the society to do so. Oliver Wendell Holmes said, "Reason means truth and those who are not governed by it take the chance that some day the sunken fact will rip the bottom out of their boat."

EXERCISE

Discuss in a small group how you would handle each of the following hypothetical cases:

1 You have a good job working for a large, prestigious company manufacturing silicon chips. Your job description includes making presentations to community organizations about the work your company is doing. Recently you have heard rumors that your company has been violating EPA (Environmental Protection Agency) regulations pertaining to the dumping of toxic wastes. You contact your supervisor and ask her if the rumors are true. She is evasive and says it doesn't affect your department and you shouldn't be concerned about it. Furthermore, she suggests that your job might be in jeopardy if you continue to pursue the matter. In the next presentation you make, a member of the audience asks you about the rumors. How do you respond?

2 A close friend of yours is applying for a job at the company where you work. Your friend asks you if you would make a personal recommendation on his behalf to the human resources manager. You go in to see the manager, and she shows you your friend's résumé and letters of application. You notice that the résumé says your friend graduated from a university that you know he never attended. The manager says that if you would like to make a recommendation, you should speak to the hiring committee. What do you do?

3 You are about to make a major presentation to a top management group regarding the safety tests that have been made on a new windshield design for automobiles. If this management group accepts your proposal, your company will be awarded a major contract and you stand to get a large bonus. You have studied this design for months and are thoroughly familiar with it. You have rehearsed the presentation a dozen times, and you are armed with a battery of handout materials and visual aids. Ten minutes before you go into the meeting, your assistant informs you that there appear to have been some mistakes made in analyzing the test results. You know that a delay would mean that the order would go to another company. Your assistant tells you that the flaws are not very bad and would probably go undetected even if the car were in an accident. What do you do?

4 You are an instructor in a college speech class. A student shows you an outline for a persuasive speech he plans to give to the class the following day. The speech advocates white supremacy and calls for the organization of an Aryan club on campus that would have as its goal discouraging black, Asian, and Mexican American students from attending. You are not able to persuade the student to change the thesis in any way. Do you allow the student to give the speech? If so, what kind of evaluation do you make?

QUESTIONS FOR REVIEW

1 What was the point made by Quintilian regarding the "good man" theory?

2 What were Aristotle's three criteria for inspiring confidence in the orator's character?

3 Why was Joseph McCarthy censured by the United States Senate? Which of Aristotle's ethical criteria did he violate?

4 What ethical infraction did Oliver North commit? What arguments did he use in his defense?

5 What is meant by the term *sophistry?* Why are sophists often able to get away with specious reasoning and unsupported claims?

6 What is the Latin phrase for "let the buyer beware"?

7 What are other arguments cited in the text that are commonly used to justify questionable ethical behavior?

8 What is meant by *utilitarian ethics?* Who was the philosopher who espoused it?

9 Describe what Richard Brandt meant by his philosophy of rule utilitarianism.

10 Who was the American author who wrote the essay "Civil Disobedience"? Who was the civil rights leader who practiced the principles described in the essay? What do we have to understand about civil disobedience before we go out and break a law we don't like?

11 What did Immanuel Kant mean by *categorical imperatives?* How does Kant's philosophy differ from that of John Stuart Mill?

12 What arguments did southerners use before the Civil War to justify slavery?

13 When Thomas Jefferson said, "All men are created equal . . . and are endowed . . . with certain unalienable rights," to whom was he referring?

14 What happened in the town of My Lai on March 16, 1968? Explain how utilitarian ethics and categorical imperatives relate to this event.

15 Describe how John Rawls of Harvard University believed the rules of society should be created.

16 What are three reasons described in the text that provide value for behaving in an ethical fashion? What are the principal responsibilities that might be included in a speaker's code of ethics?

SAMPLE SPEECH

The speech "Energy, Efficiency, Ingenuity: The Hope for the Future" was delivered by Thomas R. Kuhn, president of the Edison Electric Institute, at the company's fifty-ninth annual convention in San Diego, California, on June 5, 1991. It is reprinted here with the permission of the speaker and the publication *Vital Speeches.*

Energy, Efficiency, Ingenuity: The Hope for the Future

Thomas R. Kuhn
President, Edison Electric Institute

Delivered at the 59th Annual Convention of Edison Electric Institute, San Diego, California, June 5, 1991

Energy, Efficiency, and Ingenuity. That's our theme for this 59th Annual EEI Convention. Those same three words could also be the theme for this industry, or even for human history.

I'd like to show you why.

Let's talk about energy first.

In our industry, it's easy to think that "energy" began with Thomas Edison in 1882. We tend to make our comparisons from that point forward.

Well, 1882 may mark the beginning of the *most significant* energy era in human history, but it certainly isn't the beginning of the story. It is a fascinating story; one that we take too much for granted. And it's a story that holds important lessons for the present. Come with me on a journey into the past; you'll see what I mean.

The story begins a long, long time ago. Maybe as long as a million years ago. It begins when one of our primitive ancestors encounters a fire started by natural causes.

Experience would have taught these early humans to fear fire. But experience taught them other things, as well: that game killed in a fire tastes good; that the warmth of a fire feels good; that the light of a fire brightens the night.

Whatever the reason, on this very special occasion, curiosity overcame fear. Instead of avoiding the fire, that remote ancestor of ours approached it. Somehow he, or she, picked up a burning twig or a glowing ember and used it to make another fire. That's one theory, anyway.

We will never know who it was or even when it happened, exactly. But we know this: it was one of the most important events in the development of the human race. When our ancestor kindled that first fire, humankind became different from all of the other animals. Primitive man now controlled *two* forms of energy: his own muscle power, and fire.

The next step up the energy ladder was the use of draft animals, about 5,000 years ago. Then the wind was used to propel boats, a few hundred years later. At this point humanity had four important forms of energy: human, animal, fire, and wind. These were the foundation of early civilization.

Now, I'd like you to think about what doesn't happen next. That's right: "What *doesn't* happen next."

The last of these early energy discoveries came about 3000 B.C. Aside from the water wheel, which had limited application, no other major form of energy would be harnessed for almost 5,000 years! Moses led the Israelites out of Egypt, Alexander the Great cut the Gordian knot, Julius Caesar crossed the Rubicon, Columbus discovered the New World, Napoleon got indigestion—all with the same four energy sources.

We know that economic growth and energy use have been closely linked in modern times. Have you ever wondered if that relationship also holds up in the past? Let's take a look; let's see what happened to the standard of living during those thousands of years when energy progress stagnated.

The *Economist* magazine once calculated that there were about 250 million people on earth at the birth of Christ. They had a per capita annual income roughly equivalent to 460 of today's dollars. That was the standard of living that could be supported by human labor, assisted by animals, wind, and fire: just 460 dollars a year.

By the late 18th Century, nearly 2,000 years later, world population had increased to about 750 million. Humanity still depended on the same four forms of energy. And per capita income was still just $460. No progress in 2,000 years, in energy or income. But change was in the wind.

In the next 200 years, per capita income would increase eight-fold. World per capita income now is $3,750. In the U.S., it's about $18,000.

Think about that. No progress for thousands of years, then income jumps eight-fold in 200 years. Clearly, something big had happened; something of monumental importance. But what?

What happened is that humanity learned to control new forms of energy, and technology grew synergistically.

The progress began when coal was substituted for wood charcoal in 18th Century blast furnaces. That led to an enormous increase in iron smelting capacity.

At about the same time, the steam engine came along. Now there was a source of mechanical energy stronger than a horse and more reliable than the wind.

The steam engine opened up the coal supplies needed by the iron smelters, because it could pump water out of deep mines. It also provided the power for larger blast furnaces and further expansion of the steel industry. The steel industry and the steam engine created the railroads; the railroads created national markets.

These developments launched the Industrial Revolution at the end of the 18th Century. In the 19th, they were joined by the internal combustion engine and by electricity. Atomic energy arrived in the 20th Century.

Thanks to the cumulative impact of these new energy sources, per capita energy consumption in the U.S. today is about 327 million Btu per year. That's 96,000 kWh.

What does that mean to us? Look at it this way: The unassisted human body can do work equal to about 67 kWh per year. But each of us consumes 96,000 kWh a year. That's the equivalent of 1,433 workers. In other words, we each have 1,433 servants. That's quite a staff. Fit for a king, you might say. And those invisible servants give today's Americans not only the highest standard of living in history, but also communication, recreation, transportation, and medical care that are beyond the dreams of an Egyptian Pharaoh.

When you appreciate that, you become a little sensitive to suggestions that it's time to turn out the lights and seek a simpler lifestyle.

But to say that we value the high standard of living which energy gives us is not to say that we value waste. Far from it! That long history of energy use is a history of progress from primitive, wasteful forms of energy to more effective, more efficient forms of energy.

Which brings me to the subject of *efficiency;* that is, energy and efficiency. Like love and marriage, it's a good combination. Learning to use energy more efficiently lets us use other resources more efficiently, as well.

A water wheel could generate several hundred horsepower—more than human beings or draft animals could deliver to one place. Still, it used only a small fraction of the energy in the water flowing past it. The steam engine can produce thousands of horsepower, from wood, coal, oil, nuclear energy, or solar heat. Even so, the best of them today are less than 50 percent efficient. But the electric motor converts up to 96 percent of the energy it uses. And if you think that's impressive, don't forget the heat pump: it delivers three or four times *more* energy than it consumes. Now that's efficiency!

There are two kinds of energy efficiency: using energy more efficiently, and using more efficient energy. I am proud to say that the electric utility industry is a leader in both. Each kind of efficiency has played a role in human progress; but of the two, using more efficient energy has produced the biggest gains, by far.

Consider the history of illumination: the burning torch was followed by oil lamps and candles, then these yielded to a gas flame. Each step represents a more efficient use of the same kind of energy. And they all pale—literally—in comparison to an electric light. The electric light uses more efficient energy.

It is the *inherent efficiency* of electricity that offers the greatest potential for our energy future, but this point can be eclipsed by the wrong kind of emphasis on conservation. If conservation means using energy more efficiently, then I'm for it. But if conservation means that society should use less *electricity,* then we need to talk.

The reason is very simple: electricity can substitute for less efficient forms of energy. In doing so, energy is saved, even though *more* electricity is used.

Some people overlook that fact, because they know about conversion losses— the energy lost in converting fuel into electricity, transporting the electricity, and converting the electricity into work. I encourage them to do their homework. A little knowledge is a dangerous thing.

Look at the electric automobile. Its electric motors use electricity at about 70 percent efficiency, even after battery losses. Internal combustion automobile engines are less than 20 percent efficient. This difference in end-use energy efficiency in favor of the electric vehicle is so large that it more than offsets the energy losses at the generating plant.

Many electrotechnologies are so efficient that using them saves energy *even after allowing for conversion losses.* Here are some other examples:

—Produce steel with an electric arc instead of a blast furnace. Energy savings: 50 percent.

—Make glass with an electric melter instead of a flame. Energy savings: 65 percent.

—Dry paint with infrared electric heat rather than gas ovens. Energy savings: 90 percent.

—Cook in a microwave oven instead of a gas oven. Energy savings: 90 percent.

I could go on, but you get the idea. Remember, these big energy savings occur even after allowing for conversion losses.

Energy efficiency is desirable on economic grounds alone, but it has important environmental benefits as well. The air over our major cities today is much cleaner than it was in the 19th Century, because of the enormous gains we have made in using coal more efficiently. We can make further gains by using more efficient energy more efficiently.

If you switch to electricity to dry the paint on one car, to cook one meat loaf, to make eight glass bottles, or to produce one pound of steel, you cut production of carbon dioxide. Any *one* of these examples would cut carbon dioxide production by two pounds.

I'm not qualified to render an opinion on the effects of carbon dioxide on the global climate. But I can tell the world this: when you switch to electricity to save energy, you can also lower CO_2 production. The same is true for other pollutants. Suppose, for example, that we substitute electric vehicles for those fueled by gasoline. That would cut emissions of organic compounds and carbon monoxide by about 98 percent per vehicle, net.

Are these isolated examples, carefully selected to mask an overall efficiency deficiency? No. The benefits of using electricity that are seen at the micro level also show up economywide. Since 1973, the U.S. has increased its production of goods and services by 50 percent, while using only 9 percent more energy. The secret: a 54 percent increase in the use of electricity. At the same time, the rate of CO_2 production has dropped from four pounds per dollar of GNP in 1973 to a little more than two pounds per dollar in 1990.

Do we really want to halt progress like this, in the name of saving energy? I hope not.

I salute the environmentalists for their good intentions. But I sometimes wonder why a few of them seem so attracted to policies that would lower our standard of living; policies such as limits on electricity use. The proper objective is not a lower standard of living; it is not a "simpler life"; it is not a crusade against technology. The objective is a cleaner environment. If we can agree on that goal, then we must enlist the full force of human ingenuity in reaching it.

This brings me, finally, to *ingenuity*. Thanks to ingenuity, we use energy with efficiency. Yet, underestimating human ingenuity is one of the most persistent mistakes in history. Consider a few of these "expert" predictions from the past:

—In 10 A.D., the esteemed Roman engineer Julius Sextus Frontinus proclaimed:

> "Inventions have long since reached their limit, and I see no hope for further developments."

—In 1899, the Director of the U.S. Patent Office did it again. He advised President McKinley to close the Office, saying that

> "Everything that can be invented has been invented."

—Shortly after the birth of the airplane, the astronomer William Pickering wrote:

> "The popular mind often pictures gigantic flying machines speeding across the Atlantic carrying innumerable passengers. It seems safe to say that such ideas must be wholly visionary."

Even the greatest minds can blow it. Our own Thomas Edison once predicted:

> "Fooling around with alternating current . . . is just a waste of time. Nobody will use it, ever."

And in 1932, Albert Einstein stated:

> "There is not the slightest indication that nuclear energy will be obtainable."

These confident predictions sound funny to us now, with the benefit of hindsight. But keep in mind that they were made by leading experts of the day and seemed quite plausible at the time.

"Leading experts" still are discounting human ingenuity. The closer you come to our time, though, the more seductive their reasoning becomes.

For example, do you remember the Club of Rome? This was a group of intellectuals, technocrats, and political leaders who decided that economic growth is not sustainable. They commissioned a study to document their hunch. With the aid of computers, the study predicted that growth will be limited by the depletion of nonrenewable resources and by the accumulation of pollution. The remedy they proposed was a drastic one: stop growing.

The report of the Club of Rome was titled "The Limits to Growth." It had an enormous impact when it came out in 1971, one even greater than the impact of the "global warming" theory today. Many intellectuals and environmentalists immediately accepted the theory as fact. Who can blame them? "Running out" of resources seems inevitable. At least, it does if you fail to allow for human ingenuity.

The authors of "The Limits to Growth" were very sensitive to this criticism. They rejected it bitterly, writing that

> "Technological optimism is the most common and the most danger- ous reaction to our findings. . . ."

The problem with apocalyptic predictions like this one is that we forget about them instead of learning from the experience. They make a big splash when they come out, they may even trigger new laws, but then we forget about them. And that sets us up to be deluded by the next prophet of gloom and doom.

Well, 20 years have passed since "The Limits to Growth" was published. Just for the fun of it, let's take a look at how well those scary predictions have held up.

Here's a sample: According to "Limits," the world mined the last of its gold ore 11 years ago, the last of its mercury and silver seven years ago, and the last of its tin five years ago. Zinc ran out two years ago, we will run out of petroleum this year, and copper and lead will be exhausted next year.

Actually, the history of such predictions stretches back long before the Club of Rome. The major "improvement" added by the authors of "Limits" was the use of computers to lend a spurious credibility. As one of the study's critics commented dryly: "Malthus in, Malthus out."

Books have been written about the errors in "Limits." I don't want to beat a dead horse. But I do want to take a closer look at just one of those predictions, be- cause it makes an important point.

When the authors of "Limits" predicted that we would be running out of cop- per about now, they did it by taking the rate of copper consumption 20 years ago and increasing that consumption by the expected rate of economic growth. They could not know that by 1991 we would be replacing copper telephone wires with glass fibers. Those fibers are made from the most common element in the earth's crust and they can carry thousands of times more information than the best copper cable.

That is just one small example of the enormous impact of human ingenuity. We are constantly finding new uses for old resources, and new resources for old uses. And we are becoming more efficient—often by orders of magnitude. That's why it's risky to project consumption rates far into the future. What happens to oil con- sumption when we are all driving electric cars? What happens to air pollution? What happens to traffic congestion if we work at home and communicate by fiber optic cable?

The time may come when we will be able to make anything from anything else, given more energy. And we *will* have enough energy, if we don't lose our faith in human ingenuity.

Energy, efficiency, and ingenuity. They are the hope for the future, just as surely as they are the foundation of the past. This is our story; it is a story of progress and growth; a story we must tell others.

The road we travel is a long one; it stretches all the way back from the present to that first energy-using ancestor, and on ahead to the far horizon. I don't know what's beyond that horizon, but I'll bet on this: We will meet it head on, with a fire in our bellies, a wind in our sails, steam up, and a full charge!

INDEX

PHOTO
CREDITS

Page 1, Sven Martson/Comstock; *p. 14*, Joel Gordon; *p. 18*, Cary Wolinsky/Stock, Boston; *p. 29*, Walter S. Silver/Picture Cube; *p. 37*, Susan Lapides/Design Conceptions; *p. 45*, Joel Gordon; *p. 51*, Joseph Schuyler/Stock, Boston; *p. 62*, Hazel Hankin/Stock, Boston; *p. 71*, Susan Lapides/Design Conceptions; *p. 75*, Joel Gordon; *p. 85*, Howard Dratch/The Image Works; *p. 89*, Fredrick Bodin/Stock, Boston; *p. 97*, Lynne Jaeger Weinstein/Woodfin Camp & Associates; *p. 108*, Sven Martson/Comstock; *p. 118*, Henri Dauman/Magnum; *p. 123*, Arlene Collins/Monkmeyer; *p. 128*, Melissa Hayes English/Photo Researchers; *p. 133*, James P. Dwyer/Stock, Boston; *p. 140*, Ulrike Welsch/Photo Researchers; *p. 143*, Bob Daemmrich/Stock, Boston; *p. 147*, Irene Bayer/Monkmeyer; *p. 166*, Robert Kalman/The Image Works; *p. 171*, Tim Barnwell/Stock, Boston; *p. 181*, Sven Martson/Comstock; *p. 190*, photo supplied by the author; *p. 200*, Robert Houser/Comstock; *p. 204*, Robert Houser/Comstock.